TEN BEST IDEAS

FOR

READING
TEACHERS

EDITED BY

Edward Fry

PROFESSOR EMERITUS

RUTGERS UNIVERSITY

Addison-Wesley Publishing Company

Menlo Park, California ■ Reading, Massachusetts ■ New York

Don Mills, Ontario ■ Wokingham, England ■ Amsterdam ■ Bonn

Sydney ■ Singapore ■ Tokyo ■ Madrid ■ San Juan

Royalties accruing from the sale of this book will be paid to the Harry Singer Memorial Fellowship Fund, administered by the University of California at Riverside Foundation.

Design: Paula Shuhert

ISBN 0-201-25141-8
1 2 3 4 5 6 7 8 9 10-ML-95 94 93 92 91

Contents

Preface

This is a funny monograph. It has 44 articles all with more or less the same title: "Ten Best Ideas for Reading Teachers."

Each of the articles, however, is different, because each of the authors sees the assigned title from a different perspective and from a different background.

The origin of the project was a conference held at the University of California at Riverside and at Loyola Marymount University in Los Angeles, to pay tribute to the professional life of the late professor Harry Singer and to raise money for the scholarship held in his name. The speakers, Jay Samuels, Jeannie Chall, James Flood, and Edward Fry, donated their services, and the universities added considerable support.

The topic of the conference, Ten Best Ideas for Reading Teachers, seemed to take on an importance of its own. Each of the speakers and later, each of the invited contributors to this volume expressed an interest not only in examining their own replies but in wanting to know what the others were going to say. The rules of the game, however, were that no speaker or contributor could consult any other contributor, but had to send in their own Ten Best Ideas. The rules did allow for joint authorship, and we have several jointly authored articles by husband and wife professionals such as the Goodmans, Cunninghams, and Herbers, and several others by non-husband-and-wife teams. In one instance the whole Reading Department from Hofstra University jointly authored a Ten Best Ideas, but by and large we have single-authored articles by established reading professionals, most of whom are college professors.

In a sense, the contributions to this volume are a study of values. Each professional is exposing to the world a considered judgment based on a lifetime of study, research, and teaching. Perhaps "considered judgment" is a bit strong, as not all the authors interpreted the task in the same way. But all in all, there is a lot of "meat" in this monograph. And collectively there is an expression of many of the most important ideas in the reading field.

For those interested in survey data, approximately 165 invitations to contribute were sent out and 44 replies are published here. This gives us a response rate of 26.7%. A number of people declined to contribute by sending us a polite letter. One declination was a two-page letter, while other contributors sent us a one-page manuscript. We might even suggest that as a value study this monograph is a set of opinions at one period of time. It might be interesting to have someone repeat the survey on this same topic every decade to see how values and major trends in the reading field shift.

We confess to no scientific selection process for contributors except to say that most are active in either the International Reading Association, the National Reading Conference, or both. Most have doctorates in reading; most are, or recently have been, college professors; and nearly all have a goodly list of professional publications. In short, we wanted opinions from persons whose ideas most reading teachers would consider valuable. The choice of contributors may be slightly biased in that most are known either professionally or personally to me, but I did endeavor to get a wide variety of opinions from every corner of the nation and some from overseas. A considerable number of the contributors also knew and respected Harry Singer, who died suddenly in the fall of 1988. To those many professionals who should have been invited, I apologize, but this was just a small unfunded project that, like most projects, grew.

Definition of "Best Ideas"

Several of the contributors took it upon themselves to define the task, and I would like to share their definitions with you. Martha Rapp-Haggard Ruddell of Sonoma State University wrote:

I decided that "best" in this context means "seminal"—like a seed in being a source or in having potential for development (Webster's New World Dictionary). "Best" ideas, therefore, are ones which have generated change and/or altered the way we think about what we do; at the very least they *promise* change and evolution. These are ideas that are *important* to us—they make us better teachers and thinkers, and enrich us intellectually and practically. Further, their influence is long-standing; they have stood the test of time (or show every sign of so doing) in much the same way that classics in the arts have done. "Best" ideas give us pause to review and reexamine what we know—or what we think we know—to see if it all makes sense.

Definition of "Reading Teacher"

Another fine definition, that of a "reading teacher" was sent in by Priscilla Drum at the University of California, Santa Barbara:

The definition of a reading teacher used here is quite broad. The primary responsibility of most elementary teachers is to teach reading, particularly in grades one through three. These teachers are reading teachers, but their training in reading is often no more than a one-semester course. Those designated as reading teachers, on the other hand, have had additional training in reading methods and may have specialized in developmental or remedial instruction for elementary, secondary, or adult populations. However, these two groups, primary teachers and designated reading teachers, are not the only teachers of reading. Parents and older siblings both read to and informally instruct younger children in how to read. Friends, tutors (both trained and untrained), content area teachers, job supervisors, and craftsmen in any area also assist novices in understanding text in special areas. The most general definition of a reading teacher includes all persons who assist any nonliterate person in becoming literate or any struggling learner in better understanding a text in a new domain of knowledge.

Contents

The contributors were told that their submissions could be anything from one page to a short article. The only format constraint was that they had to include the numerals from 1 to 10. Because of limitations of space we were forced to shorten some submissions, but by and large, the writing was exceptionally good. Of course, that is what one might expect when one of the selection criteria was that they be well-published authors. We did allow the conference speakers somewhat more space, and these articles appear first. All other authors are inserted alphabetically.

Most authors submitted ten ideas, but there are some exceptions. Two writers, Squire and Binkley, each sent in just one idea. Since I usually identify myself as an author, I found it interesting that the two people who bent the rules the furthest are both editors.

It is difficult to generalize about the contents, as each author viewed his or her task differently and, as we mentioned, was forbidden to contact everyone else. However, there are several broad divisions.

One division is between those papers that concentrated on "seminal" ideas and the more practical papers that gave actual teaching suggestions. Incidentally, some people that I consider hard-core researchers like

Carver and Venezky came down on the practical side.

Another division might be seen between the more general Best Ideas and those aimed at a specific method or population. For example, Chall chose to aim her ideas at the disadvantaged underachievers or what are now called "children at risk," while Balajthy aimed at computer usage in reading, and Kress chose to talk to teacher trainers.

Because reading is so vital a part of the language learning process for language-minority students, many of the Best Ideas are especially appropriate for teachers of English as a Second Language. Crawford speaks directly to a language-minority population, and Alvermann, Estes, Schell, and Stanchfield list ideas that would be very helpful with ESL students. But in general good reading ideas apply to ESL students just as well as they do to native English-speaking students.

Most of the Best Ideas apply to reading in general or to elementary reading, but there are at least some aimed at secondary and college reading, such as the articles by Rabin, Donlan, and Stahl, Simpson and Hayes. Within the articles themselves there is somewhat of a division between traditional ideas, such as the importance of vocabulary or phonics, and newer trends such as the importance of incorporating writing and schema theory influences. But enough of these comments on contents. See for yourself. Read the whole thing, or just dabble around among favorite authors. There are some wonderful, exciting ideas in here. Some are ideas you may have just forgotten and some are ideas you have never heard of, but collectively they can cause you to examine your own value system as to what really are the Ten Best Ideas for Reading Teachers.

—Edward Fry

Acknowledgments

First, I would like to thank the original conference speakers, Jay Samuels, Jeannie Chall, and James Flood. If they hadn't come to Southern California and talked to two large interested audiences of reading teachers, this project would never have gotten off the ground.

Next, I would like to thank the many authors who contributed to this monograph. They are all busy people with many demands on their time. While some of them were kind enough to say that they found the assigned title of coming up with their Ten Best Ideas was interesting and challenging, I know that it still took work, time, and effort, plus a willingness to be exposed before their peers. In fact some of them said, "I can't wait to see what the others have selected as their Ten Best Ideas." A few have said that they hope to use such a volume in one of their classes so that their students can be exposed to a variety of ideas (not just the Best Ideas of the instructor).

A hearty vote of thanks is also in order to the University of California at Riverside and the Dean of Education, Irving Hendrick, and his Associate Dean, Dan Donlan. They really supplied much of the funds for this "unfunded project" in the form of secretarial services, stamps, phones, offices, and many supporting services.

But the biggest thanks belongs to Sara (Sally) Beach, my trusty editorial assistant, who was a major force in editing and piloting the manuscript through to completion. Ms. Beach is a doctoral candidate in reading at UCR and can rightfully lay claim to being Harry Singer's last doctoral student. I know that she and many others who contributed to this volume did so partly for him.

Jeanne S. Chall

HARVARD UNIVERSITY

I believe that the most serious reading problem today is the low level of literacy of children in the United States, particularly among about one-third of our children and young people, those increasingly referred to as children "at risk." Why are they achieving poorly? And how can we improve their achievement?

Tens of millions of children in the United States have problems in learning to read; their achievement lags behind national norms, and the lags increase the longer they are in school. This group includes children from low-income families, ethnic minorities, children in inner cities, non-English-speaking or limited speakers of English, and those with specific reading and learning disabilities. Taken together, various estimates indicate that they may now make up about a third or more of the school population. And according to demographic predictions, their numbers are growing (Chall, 1985).

Let us take one part of this one third — those with severe reading and learning disabilities, often referred to as having dyslexia. There is general agreement among researchers that from 10 to 15 percent of the population is so handicapped. Their reading achievement lags significantly behind their mental ability and language comprehension. Although improved classroom instruction makes it easier for them to learn to read, their difficulties often persist and take different forms as they progress. They *can* learn, and they do, when they receive proper diagnosis and remediation. And the earlier they are given these, the better they do (Chall and Peterson, 1986).

Thus, in order to effect a significant improvement in the reading of children with reading/learning disabilities, we will need to provide the resources for diagnosis and treatment and seek also for the ways to prevent or alleviate the severity of their difficulties in the regular classroom.

My ten fundamental concepts are concerned with helping teachers understand the problems of children who lag behind the norms, and helping teachers and administrators make the early decisions that can prevent and alleviate reading difficulties for those children.

1   I select three fundamental concepts that I think are most helpful for finding and understanding those with reading/learning disabilities. My first choice is one of the oldest concepts in the psychology of

reading—standardized reading tests. Many people are critical of tests today, and too often tests are blamed for the misuses made of them. But they do have constructive uses, and one is to tell us early whether children are reading as well as they should for their age and grade. In our quest for ever more "true" and "qualitative" evaluations we may overlook the value of benchmarks — or norms — that alert us as to whether to worry or not to worry. Most medical examinations are based on norms and, as parents, we would not be satisfied with a diagnosis only that our child is doing nicely, is improving. We would want to know how far our child is from the norm.

The concept of norms in reading achievement is one of the earliest and most enduring concepts in the psychology and teaching of reading. Tests may change, they may improve, but essentially I believe that *the concept of norms, or progression, of a child's achievement in relation to grade and age norms is a valuable concept*—particularly for helping those students who test below the norms. This is an alert, a sign that something may be off; something needs our attention. The test may not tell what that is, but a whistle was blown.

2   My second concept is also an old one—and one that, if used with understanding and sensitivity, also helps us understand the needs of children with reading/learning disabilities. I refer to *estimates of a child's reading potential*—tests or observations that help us estimate whether reading skills are on a par with cognitive abilities. These may be estimated by individually-administered intelligence tests (WISC, Stanford-Binet), listening comprehension tests, orally-administered vocabulary tests, and so on. Most children with reading/learning disabilities do better on such aptitude tests than on reading achievement tests. Indeed, these aptitude tests alert us to the fact that they can be doing better and need help (Chall and Curtis, 1987).

3   My third reading concept, again classic since it was discovered nearly 100 years ago, is that remediation, or special reading help, given to children who present a gap between potential and achievement, works—and the benefits are both short-term and long-term. *Remedial reading—or its many new names—reading recovery, developmental reading, Chapter 1, resource rooms, that is, instruction geared to the strengths and weaknesses of those with reading/learning disabilities—works!* Of course,

the better the remediation, the better the results. And the earlier the remediation, the more effective it is (Smith, 1979).

My seven remaining fundamental concepts in reading can help us understand and solve the reading problems of children of low-income families and also raise the level of proficiency of all children and young people.

4   My fourth concept is the conception of reading as changing as it develops. *Although we use only one word for "reading," what it stands for changes qualitatively as the reader matures* from the earliest stage of showing curiosity about print and books, to reading simple familiar texts, to mature reading of different kinds of texts that contain unfamiliar, complex ideas written in difficult language.

One of the major changes comes at about the fourth grade, when the texts read become more difficult, are on unfamiliar topics, and use language that is increasingly more complex. This is in contrast to the reading task of the first three grades, which is essentially that of reading familiar texts—using high frequency, concrete words already within students' understanding. At fourth grade the reading task changes. The texts read in schools and outside contain more unfamiliar ideas and more abstract, technical, and specialized vocabularies (Chall, 1983).

Viewing reading as changing makes it possible for us to explain why low-income children score close to national norms in grades 1 to 3, but score below average after grade 4. They have the language necessary for reading in the early grades. But their abstract and technical vocabularies do not keep up with the reading demands at grade 4 and beyond, unless the teachers provide for it (Chall, Jacobs, and Baldwin, 1990). Mainstream children, on the other hand, have a greater chance of learning abstract and technical words at home, from books read to them and from reading on their own.

5   *Readability theory and measurement also help explain the increasing difficulty with reading* and writing that low-income children have in successive grades. Readability measurement has found consistently for more than 70 years that vocabulary difficulty is the best predictor of comprehension difficulty. Indeed, it is at about a fourth grade readability level that

one is able to write serious content using words that are beyond the most elemental, concrete, and frequent in the language (Chall,1984).

6 My sixth concept is that *reading at any level can be viewed as composed of three components—language, cognition, and reading skills* (Carroll, 1977). In the early grades all children are stronger in language and cognition than in reading skills, which are virtually non-existent. The task of reading instruction in the first few grades, therefore, is to teach children to recognize and decode the words they already know when they hear them. By grade 4, most children's word recognition and decoding skills have caught up sufficiently to their language and cognition so that they can recognize and sound out most words—even those whose meanings they do not know. Thus, the task of reading beginning at about grade 4 becomes mainly one of acquiring a broader and deeper vocabulary and reasoning ability applied to reading.

7 Seventh, *it is important both to learn reading skills and to practice using them on a great variety of texts in different situations* (Chall, 1987a).

8 Eighth, *a degree of challenge is essential for continued progress.* Teacher-directed instruction in reading should be challenging—not too easy, not too hard. If it is always within the ability of students, they will not make as great progress (Chall, 1987b).

9 Ninth, *vocabulary, or actually two vocabularies, are critical to reading comprehension.* In the primary grades, the child's main task is to learn to recognize words. And in the intermediate grades and beyond, meanings become more important. Every study of reading at grade 4 and beyond shows that vocabulary is the strongest factor in comprehension (Thorndike, 1973-74; Chall and Stahl, 1985). Once decoding is learned, a good meaning vocabulary means good comprehension; a limited page vocabulary usually means poor comprehension (Chall, 1987c). Thus every teacher should be a teacher of vocabulary.

10 Since vocabulary is acquired also from wide reading, my tenth concept is *the importance of reading a wide variety of reading materials.* They should be available and accessible in classrooms as well as in school and public libraries, and should include books, newspapers, magazines, dictionaries, encyclopedias, and more—on a wide variety

of topics, genres, and difficulty levels (Chall and Snow, 1988; Chall, Jacobs, and Baldwin, 1990). These materials are needed not only for teaching students how to read but for showing them what it truly means to read—to share in the knowledge, joys and pains of our times and times past.

Edward Fry

UNIVERSITY OF CALIFORNIA, RIVERSIDE

1   *Reading ability follows the normal curve.*

All kinds of evidence is available showing that reading ability follows the normal curve, including state tests, commercial standardized tests (like the CTBS), college entrance tests (like the SAT and ACE), and the National Assessment of Educational Progress. You can even see it in your own class or your own school by just giving a simple vocabulary test using random words from a school dictionary. Raw scores from any of these tests can then be plotted on a graph to show you the curve, and if you desire you can calculate grade-equivalent scores, percentiles or other scores.

Look at Figure 1 and Figure 2 showing a normal spread of reading abilities for a fourth grade and for a ninth grade.

Note that it is "normal" to have 4 fourth graders reading at a second-grade level or below, and conversely it is normal to have 4 fourth graders reading at sixth-grade level or above.

A similar phenomenon occurs at the ninth grade, except that the standard deviation and range are wider. One out of seven ninth graders (16%) read at sixth-grade level or below and one out of seven read at twelfth-grade level or above. Incidentally, the ninth-grade reading ability curve is somewhere near the United States adult reading ability distribution.

If your school is located in a low socio-economic area, the median and all the scores will shift down. If your school is in an above-average socio-economic area, the median and all the scores shift upwards.

What does this mean to reading teachers? It means that they must be aware of the way children come to school and plan for and expect individual differences. All the school resources shouldn't be concentrated on the lowest quartile, because those children in the middle and upper quartiles deserve their fair share of educational effort. No student or group of students, whatever their ability, should be ignored.

2   *Reading is developmental.*

Children learn to read harder and harder material as they progress through the school years. All tests and common experience show this.

Figure 1 The Normal Distribution Curve

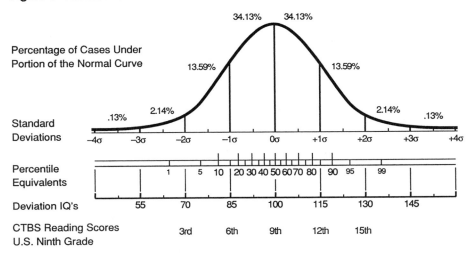

Percentage of Cases Under Portion of the Normal Curve

34.13% 34.13%

13.59% 13.59%

.13% 2.14% 2.14% .13%

Standard Deviations

-4σ -3σ -2σ -1σ 0σ +1σ +2σ +3σ +4σ

Percentile Equivalents

1 5 10 20 30 40 50 60 70 80 90 95 99

Deviation IQ's

55 70 85 100 115 130 145

CTBS Reading Scores U.S. Ninth Grade

3rd 6th 9th 12th 15th

In a typical ninth grade 1 out of 7 (16%) students read at sixth-grade level or below. Also 1 out of 7 read at twelfth-grade level or above.

In a low socio-economic status school the median on all the scale shifts down one or two grade levels and in a high socio-economic status school the median shifts up.

Figure 2 The Normal Distribution Curve Translated Into a Typical Fourth Grade of 32 Children

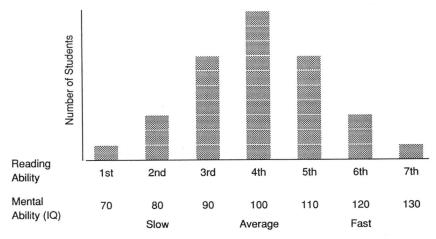

Number of Students

Reading Ability

1st 2nd 3rd 4th 5th 6th 7th

Mental Ability (IQ)

70 80 90 100 110 120 130

Slow Average Fast

Note that it is "normal" to have 4 fourth graders reading at second-grade level or below. Conversely you should have 4 reading at sixth-grade level or above. In a democracy it is the teacher's job to move *every* child up a notch or two whether the child is slow, average, or fast.

P.S. You can't get all children "up to grade level."

Slow children do progress, and fast children progress faster. This concept has been refined by some reading experts, such as Singer and Donlan (1989) in their discussion of "reading to learn versus learning to read" and Jeannie Chall (1983) with her famous "stages" of reading development.

It is nearly impossible to talk meaningfully about children or adults who "can't read" or are illiterate. Everybody is somewhere along a continuum of reading ability. There are nearly as many definitions of literacy as definers. For example, the U.S. Census for many years defined literacy as having five or more years of schooling. UNESCO defines world literacy as the ability to read and write a simple sentence. The U.S. high school equivalency test (GED) requires about eighth-grade reading ability. Most adults can read something even if it is only a STOP sign, and at the other extreme, most adults are illiterate when it comes to reading theoretical physics.

3 Materials are developmental.

Beginning readers do better with easier materials. By "doing better" we mean that comprehension of the materials will be better, reading lessons will be more successful, and pleasure will be greater if there is at least a rough match between the reader's ability and the difficulty of the reading material. Reading material can be graded approximately using a readability formula. A person's reading ability can be judged using formal and informal tests. Thus a reading teacher, or anybody selecting reading material, must have some awareness of the difficulty of the material and the reading ability of the intended reader. Plenty of evidence is available to show that unless motivation is extremely high, the too-difficult material will cause a loss of comprehension, an increase in oral reading errors, and an inclination to stop reading. See Figures 3 and 4.

4 SES is correlated with reading achievement.

Socio-economic status (SES) can be measured a number of ways, including amount of parent education or income. The National Assessment of Educational Progress and all the major standardized tests show that there is a high correlation between reading achievement scores and SES for most groups. This fact does not mean that there are not brilliant readers in the slums, or poor readers in the exurbs, because the normal distribution curve operates both places.

Figure 3 Graph for Estimating Readability: Extended

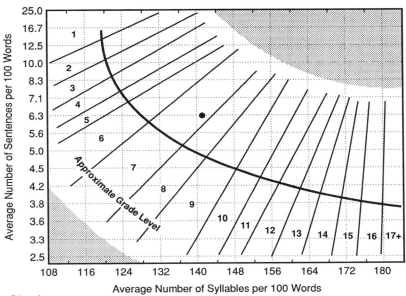

Average Number of Syllables per 100 Words

Directions:

Randomly select 3 one-hundred-word passages from a book or article. Plot the average number of sylllables and average number of sentences per 100 words on the graph to determine the grade level of the material. Choose more passages per book if great variability is observed and conclude that the book has uneven readability. Few books will fall in the gray area, but when they do, grade level scores are invalid.

Count proper nouns, numerals, and initializations as words. Count a sylllable for each symbol. For example, "1945" is 1 word and 4 sylllables, and "IRA" is 1 word and 3 syllables.

Example:

	Syllables	Sentences
First Hundred Words	124	6.6
Second hundred Words	141	5.5
Third Hundred Words	158	6.8
Average	141	6.3

Readability Seventh Grade (see dot plotted on graph)

For further information see the *Journal of Reading*, January 1989 or December 1977.

9

Figure 4

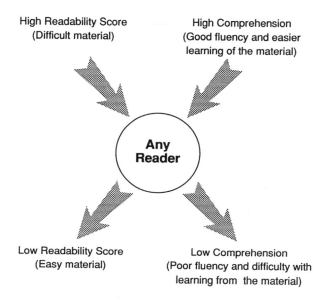

High Readability Score (Difficult material)

High Comprehension (Good fluency and easier learning of the material)

Any Reader

Low Readability Score (Easy material)

Low Comprehension (Poor fluency and difficulty with learning from the material)

What it does mean is that the low SES schools will have lower mean scores and many more poor readers (a whole lower normal curve), so the schools or the teachers shouldn't be blamed, because the problem is bigger than they can handle. This SES correlation points out the importance of parents in the reading process. It is vital to have books in the home and to read to children starting at a very young age.

5 *A variety of methods work.*

I'm almost ashamed not to know which is the best method to teach reading. Not only that, I don't know anybody who does. I do know many methods that work. And I have seen plenty of people who discover some method new to them who temporarily or permanently think that it is the best method. But when you get right down to selecting the "best" method for a class or a school or a state and you try to scientifically evaluate the results after a few years by using several good tests or any objective method (not personal opinions) and a large experimental and control group, you have trouble showing that there is one best method. If you doubt this, take a look at the First Grade Studies (Bond and Dykstra, 1967). Twenty-seven different university investigators used beginning reading methods ranging from supposedly pure phonics to whole word (meaning emphasis on traditional basals), language experience approach (now called the whole language method), or funny alphabets like the ITA or modified alphabets like the DMS. Certainly no method came out head and shoulders above any other, nor did any method fail to teach reading. At best, there were tenths of a grade differences among methods after one, two, or three years of teaching. Not only that, but no particular method was best for any subgroup such as boys/girls or high/low ability.

What did occur was plenty of variability between classrooms, which lends some credence to the notion that good teachers make a difference. These findings also suggest that perhaps every teacher should be allowed to use any recognized method of teaching reading she chooses as long as she is getting good results.

6 *Vocabulary knowledge is highly correlated to reading comprehension.*

If research is a little mushy on methods, it is beautiful and clean on vocabulary. First of all, there is a wealth of evidence to indicate that a high correlation exists between vocabulary knowledge and reading comprehension. Every standardized test shows it; factor analysis studies like those by Davis (1968) and the substrata factor analysis by Holmes and his students (1953) show it, and many other studies like the First Grade Studies mentioned earlier also show it. Not only that, but you can improve a student's vocabulary by teaching words, which implies that vocabulary should be taught—as a part of a reading lesson, as part of a mathematics lesson, as part of a science lesson, as part of physical education— well, you get the idea.

Another important part of vocabulary teaching is the fine research done on word frequency counts and word knowledge studies. First, the word frequency counts from the classic studies by psychologist Edward Thorndike (1921) down to the American Heritage study done by John Carroll and others (1971) all tend to show one startling fact—a small number of words account for a high percentage of all reading material. If you take a high frequency list like my Instant Words (which are a modification of the American Heritage 5 million word count), you will find that just the first hundred Instant Words account for 50% of all written material. That's right, half of the *New York Times* and half of your second-grade text are composed of just 100 words. Unfortunately, it is a declining curve, so 200 words won't give you 100% but 300 Instant Words will account for 65%, on the average, of all written material. The obvious conclusion is that every reader must know those 300 words, and not just know them, but recognize them instantly in order to free up his or her brain for the more important task of comprehension.

A list of the 100 Instant Words appears in Figure 5. They can be taught by lots of easy reading, flash cards, games, writing experiences, spelling lessons, or any way you want, but a good reader must know them. Don't try to teach them all at once.

In case you want the most common 1000 words in English for your reading or writing (spelling) lessons, see *The New Reading Teachers Book of Lists* (Fry, Fountoukidis, and Polk, 1984). These words make up about 90% of all written materials.

The word knowledge research headed by Dale and O'Rourke (1976) shows the words, by meaning, that are known at each grade level. This is important data which unfortunately is not usually used in developing curriculum materials.

7 Background knowledge affects comprehension.

It almost goes without saying that comprehension is the ultimate goal of all reading. It is why we use all the methods, why we use phonics, why we use a high frequency vocabulary, and why we use direct comprehension instruction. So comprehension is important. Keep teaching it every way you can.

However, a relatively new approach to comprehension has appeared on the reading comprehension scene in the last decade under the loose name of *schema theory*. This important trend emphasizes the necessity of readers' background for reading comprehension. All kinds of previous experience are good. Personal experiences, culture, wide reading, good TV programs, and education in many subjects all contribute to background knowledge.

One practical outcome of schema theory has been the graphic

Figure 5   The First 100 Instant Words

These are the most often used words in reading and writing. They are listed in order of frequency in Columns 1 through 4. Make sure your student knows most of these before teaching the second 100. Teach only a few at a time to keep the success rate high.

Column 1 Words 1 to 25	Column 2 Words 26-50	Column 3 Words 51-75	Column 4 Words 75-100
the	or	will	number
of	one	up	no
an	had	other	way
a	by	about	could
to	words	out	people
in	but	many	my
is	not	then	than
you	what	them	first
that	all	these	water
it	were	so	been
he	we	some	called
was	when	her	who
for	your	would	oil
on	can	make	its
are	said	like	now
as	there	him	find
with	use	into	long
his	an	time	down
they	each	has	day
I	which	look	did
at	she	two	get
be	do	more	come
this	how	write	made
have	their	go	may
from	if	see	part

mapping or networking of concepts (Pearson and Johnson, 1978). These diagrams show the interrelatedness of different concepts and the richness of concepts that can be associated with a new concept. Mapping is also an important tool in vocabulary building. Figures 6 and 7 show one type of semantic map or cognitive map that can be used in teaching new vocabulary terms or reading concepts. Study the filled-in illustration to make it more meaningful. The map is for comparing and contrasting two terms on the coordinate level, but a simpler map, having just one term on the coordinate level, can be used. It is based on the ideas of Pearson and Johnson.

8 *Sounds do correlate to symbols.*

We read an alphabetic language. In theory an alphabet is a set of symbols that stand for speech sounds. Over the centuries, however, our alphabet's fit, or sound-symbol correspondence, has become a little distorted. Teaching phonics is still important because phonetic analysis, or decoding, is one important way to learn new words as well as a way to learn to spell. Modern phonics systems are an improvement over those used in past times like the inaccurate systems taught in the New England Primer and the McGuffey readers. Knowing some phonics also helps more mature readers to use any dictionary pronunciation system.

9 *Reading worthwhile content provides meaningful purpose for reading.*

Recently a lot of emphasis has been placed on what children read. The trend toward using good children's authors in basal readers and the use of trade books and classic literature as part of the reading curriculum is all to the good. Modern textbooks also show sensitivity for the diversity of our school population so that reading books and textbooks tend to be more interracial, nonsexist, and multicultural than they were in the past. Reading teachers should also be careful that the content is not all narration (stories) to the exclusion of expository prose.

10 *Organization of the reading field provides ready resources for teachers.*

In the last half century the reading field has become highly organized.

Figure 6

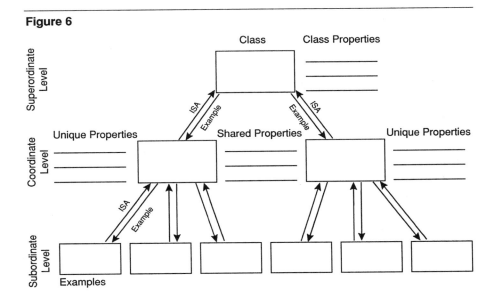

Superordinate Level

Class   Class Properties

ISA   Example   Example   ISA

Coordinate Level

Unique Properties   Shared Properties   Unique Properties

ISA   Example

Subordinate Level

Examples

Figure 7

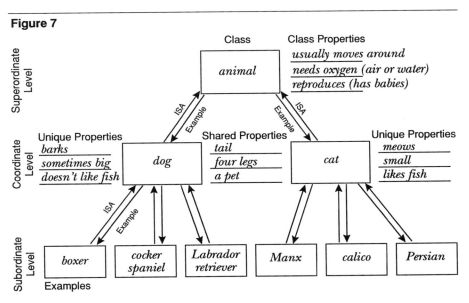

Superordinate Level

Class   Class Properties

animal

usually moves around
needs oxygen (air or water)
reproduces (has babies)

ISA   Example   Example   ISA

Coordinate Level

Unique Properties
barks
sometimes big
doesn't like fish

dog

Shared Properties
tail
four legs
a pet

cat

Unique Properties
meows
small
likes fish

ISA   Example

Subordinate Level

boxer   *cocker spaniel*   *Labrador retriever*   *Manx*   *calico*   *Persian*

Examples

This illustration compares and contrasts the vocabulary terms "dog" and "cat" for better understanding and enrichment. Note that a boxer "isa" dog and a dog "isa" animal (arrows going up) and an "example" of an animal is a dog (arrows going down give examples). The examples on the subordinate level could also have properties. Also note that each term has all the properties of the higher class. For example, a dog has all the properties of an animal, but shares only some properties with a cat, which is on the same (coordinate) level. Maps like these are excellent for answering those important concept (schema) building questions, "How are these two things alike and how are they different?"

It is hard to realize that the International Reading Association was only founded in 1955 and now has chapters in every state, a thousand local chapters, and national organizations in over 40 countries. Each unit holds meetings for self education and a professional exchange of ideas on teaching reading, and many have publications as well. Other organizations are devoted to specialized areas of reading, such as research (National Reading Conference) or college teaching (College Reading Association).

Most colleges and universities have expanded reading education from the old days when it was just part of a language arts course to special reading courses for most preservice teachers, plus master's degrees, specialist degrees, and doctoral degrees in reading education. Most states also issue some type of professional certification for reading teachers.

Printed material for the reading field has also greatly expanded. Modern reading series have more books and materials and are much better organized and graded than they were a half century ago. The number of trade books available has greatly increased. Reading tests, both formal and informal, are better. The amount of supplemental reading material is enormous and varies from traditional drill books and workbooks to computer aided instruction.

This better organization of professional associations, of teacher education, and of materials has in turn helped the reading teacher to be better organized.

S. Jay Samuels

UNIVERSITY OF MINNESOTA

1 Phasing Out the Teacher and Phasing in the Learner

This idea came from Harry Singer, who believed that teachers should empower students by gradually transferring to the students the knowledge of how to be independent as a student and as a scholar. Teachers know how to ask good questions, know how to analyze what is important in a text, know how to read for meaning, know how to synthesize information, and know how to conduct a good discussion. Why not transfer this knowledge to the students and train them on how to manage their own discussions? While we give lip service to the idea that our goal as educators is to educate our students so that they will be independent learners, unless we phase out the teacher and phase in the learner, many of our students will fail to become independent because throughout their education they were always placed in a dependent role — dependent on the teacher.

2 Stages in Learning a Skill

Research on learning shows that there are two definite stages: developing accuracy and then developing automaticity. It has been well known that the first stage shows large individual differences in the amount of time necessary for acquiring a skill, differences which are often related to intelligence. A new finding is that while there are still individual differences in development of automaticity, these are significantly smaller than in the first stage. In other words, the more intelligent student becomes accurate sooner than the less intelligent student. Once the student is highly accurate, however, he or she becomes automatic in about the same period of time. (See Figure 1.)

What are the implications of this exciting new finding about the small differences in the time it takes to become automatic? It means that once a student can be brought to the stage of accuracy, that virtually all students can achieve automaticity, or fluency. Thus, the teacher's tasks are: first, motivating the students so that they stay on task long enough to become accurate, and two, motivating the students so that they practice until they become automatic, or fluent.

Figure 1 Learning Curves for Speed and Accuracy

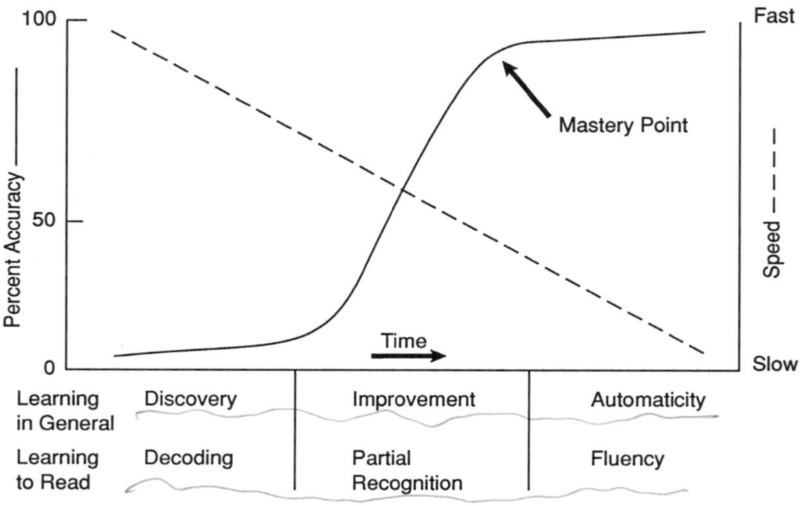

NOTE: Speed continues to improve after mastery (high accuracy). The implication for reading teachers is that more practice or repeated readings are necessary even after mastery (100% accuracy) on any new difficulty level.

3 Teaching Word Recognition Skills

While we all agree that the end product of reading is comprehension, a necessary prerequisite is the ability to recognize words. Regardless of whether one uses a whole-language approach or a research-based eclectic approach to reading, most students will require instruction in how to recognize words, and to this end, direct explicit instruction is most valuable.

4 Automaticity and Repeated Reading

Previously, I discussed the importance of automaticity as a stage in learning. How does one become automatic in reading? At the present time, the only way we know is through practice. In order to encourage students to become automatic at word recognition, what the teacher should do is to encourage students to read as much easy material as possible. In reading as in other matters, "practice makes perfect."

A proven technique for building automaticity is to use the method of repeated reading. This method simply has the student read and reread a short story or part of a story until it can be read with some

18

degree of speed and expression, and with few word recognition errors. When the goals of page speed and word recognition accuracy are reached, the student repeats the process with a new selection.

5 Direct Teaching of Comprehension

By now it is well established that teachers tend to assess comprehension rather than to teach it. While it is important to evaluate how well the student is doing, it is also important to teach comprehension skills. Without direct and explicit instruction in higher-order reasoning and thinking, some students will not learn these skills.

6 Text Structure of Narrative and Expository Texts

While all students are aware that a building has a structure, not all students are aware of text structure, especially expository text structure. By providing instruction in text structure and showing students how they can use this knowledge when reading for learning and for recall, teachers can help students improve comprehension and memory for text.

7 Depth of Processing

Depth of processing refers to the kind of mental activities we engage in as we try to learn and remember. For example, assume that I wanted students to recall the following words: *bank, government, deity, illuminate,* and *shelter.* What if one group of students was told to write each of the words twice while a second group was told to find a synonym for each word and then to use each word in a sentence? Depth of processing theory states that group two should remember the words better because they were required to process at the level of meaning while the first group was processing at a surface non-meaning level. The classroom implication of this theory is that to enhance learning and memory we should have students make sense of what they are reading by asking them to engage in activities such as synthesizing information, making predictions, finding analogies, summarizing, and finding applications and examples.

8 Readability Research

Readability research is important because it helps teachers understand what text elements contribute to text comprehension difficulties. It also helps teachers select reading material that is appropriate for the level of reading ability of their classes.

9 Metacognition

There are several aspects to metacognition. In part it refers to the reader's self-awareness of a breakdown in comprehension. In part it also refers to the strategies available to the reader for solving a comprehension problem. Since all readers experience problems in comprehension from time to time, it is essential that they know how to monitor their own reading and also know how to self-correct. Good readers have better metacognitive abilities than poor readers, and the monitoring and self-correcting skills are teachable.

10 Integrating Language Arts

Reading pedagogy has come full circle. In the early and mid-1800s reading, spelling, and writing were usually taught together. Then in the early 1900s there was a separation of these skills. Now we are witnessing the rejoining of the related language arts, and this change is considered to be a positive move because the combination is considered to be synergistic; that is, each skill helps the other. Combining language arts is more time efficient and more efficient from the vantage point of learning.

James Flood and Diane Lapp

SAN DIEGO STATE UNIVERSITY

In the past few years, a great deal has been written about "state-of-the-art" reading comprehension instructional practices (Cunningham and Tierney, 1984); (Duffy, Roehler, and Mason, 1983); (Durkin, 1978-79); (Flood, 1984a, 1984b); (Guthrie, 1981); (Pearson, 1982, 1985); (Pearson and Gallagher, 1983); (Robinson et al., 1989). In each of these writings, the authors have maintained that comprehension instruction is dependent upon the interaction of four sets of critical variables: *reader variables* (age, ability, affect, motivation), *text variables* (genre, type, features, considerateness); *educational-context variables* (environment, task, social grouping, purpose); and *teacher variables* (knowledge, experience, attitude and pedagogical approach); and that each of these variables needs to be taken into consideration when designing an effective approach to comprehension instruction.

An Instructional Approach: Constructivism Put Into Practice

It has been argued that students develop comprehension skills and strategies most successfully through a process approach that emphasizes the underlying cognitive and linguistic skills that are prerequisites for understanding and appreciating texts (Anderson et al., 1985; Flood, 1984a, 1984b; Holbrook, 1987; Lapp and Flood, 1986; Rumelhart, 1984). Just as has been the case for some time in writing instruction, reading instruction is undergoing a profound change in its theoretical orientation and ensuing pedagogy. Educators are moving away from approaches in which reading is taught as a series of fragmented subskills to a holistic approach in which comprehension is viewed as a unitary process (Robinson et al., 1989). As a result, contemporary comprehension instruction needs to be based on constructivist principles which acknowledge the student's role as the meaning-maker in the reading act.

What are the instructional implications of such an approach? Can constructivism be the basis for effective instruction in which students learn to internalize rules and strategies for comprehending? Applebee (1991) argues that it can be—if there is a shift from the metaphor of "diagnosis and prescription" that has been used traditionally to discuss teaching and learning to a new metaphor that adequately advances a constructivist notion of teaching and learning. Applebee argues for the use of instructional scaffolding as the most fitting metaphor for teaching and learning, suggesting that it more fully describes teaching and learning because it focuses on the notion of dynamic learning within a specific context. The metaphor of instructional scaffolding supports a process-oriented approach that perceives the teacher's role as one that provides necessary and meaningful support, and the student's role as one that is itself the maker of meaning. The notion of "instructional scaffolding" requires the student to take ownership for learning and the teacher to provide appropriate direction and support. It is a form of collaboration between teachers and students in which teachers and students work together to ensure that students internalize rules and strategies for meaning-making.

Ten Practices That Foster Constructivist Principles

There are many teaching and learning activities that foster constructivist notions and lead to the development of comprehension abilities. These activities are based on the premise that comprehension is a gradual, emerging process in which students grow in comprehension abilities by processing texts in a generative manner, building on their own experiences, knowledge and values. Ten practices that have been proven successful in helping students develop their comprehension abilities will be discussed. These include:

1. Preparing for Reading Practices,
2. Reciprocal Teaching Practices,
3. Understanding and Using Narrative Text Structure Knowledge Practices,
4. Understanding and Using Expository Text Structure Knowledge Practices,
5. Questioning Practices,
6. Inference Question Training Practices,
7. Information Processing Practices,
8. Developing Analogies Practices,
9. Summarizing Practices, and
10. Voluntary/Recreational Reading Practices.

1 Preparing for Reading Practices

Three activities that help students ready themselves for reading are PReP, Previewing, and Anticipation Guides.

Prereading Plan (PReP)

Langer (1982, 1984) proposed an activity that prepares students for reading by activating their prior knowledge through a series of prompt questions. There are three stages to PReP:

a. initial associations;

b. reflections about initial associations; and

c. reformulation of knowledge.

In the initial association stage, the teacher selects a word, phrase, or picture about the key concept in the text and initiates a discussion to induce concept-related associations. For example, in teaching a lesson about the American Revolution, the teacher might ask, "What comes to mind when you hear the words 'Revolutionary War'?" During the reflection stage students are asked to explain their associations. The teacher might ask, "Why do those ideas come to mind?" Langer (1984) found that the social context of this activity advanced students' understanding—they expanded and/or revised their knowledge through listening to and interacting with their peers. In the final stage, reformulation of knowledge, students might be asked, "Have you gained any new information about the Revolutionary War?" Langer found that students' knowledge was expanded through the generative processes in which they were engaged. She found that students' responses changed from remotely related personal experiences to an understanding of relations between pieces of knowledge.

Previewing

Graves and Penn (1985) tested a procedure in which students listened to a lengthy preview of an assigned text. The preview was prepared by the teacher and its purpose was to motivate students. It had three parts:

a. the activation of prior personal experiences that were relevant to the text;

b. the building of necessary background knowledge for the text; and

c. the establishment of an organizational framework for the text that was consistent with the framework the author used to present information.

Students who listened to the previews before reading the text significantly outperformed students who did not have previews on multiple measures of comprehension.

Anticipation Guides

Herber (1978) designed a previewing guide in which students were encouraged to predict the information that they expected to encounter in the text. As they read the text, their predictions were compared with the information that was actually contained in the text. This active form of processing text helped children develop effective comprehension strategies and enhanced their overall knowledge of the text.

2 Reciprocal Teaching Practices

Palincsar and Brown (1982, 1985) and Palincsar (1984) have developed a paradigm that has been effective for developing constructivist, process-oriented reading comprehension abilities. In their methodology, students and teachers take turns assuming the role of the teacher through a structured dialogue. The teacher models four distinct comprehension strategies and the students have opportunities to practice these strategies. Students are asked to

a. summarize the paragraph that was read in a simple sentence,

b. generate a question for a fellow student about the paragraph that was read,

c. ask for clarity (or resolution) of anything in the text that was unclear, and

d. make a prediction about what will happen next in the text.

In the studies, students were shown how to use these strategies by teacher modeling. Adult support was withdrawn gradually as students exhibited their ability to perform the task independently. Palincsar (1984) reported gains of 35% and more on comprehension assessments after twenty days of instruction.

Palincsar and Brown's (1982) original formulation was based on

24

Vygotsky's notions about the zone of proximal development which he described as:

> The distance between the actual developmental level as determined by independent problem solving and the level of potential development as determined through problem solving under adult guidance or in collaboration with more capable peers.

The foundation of Palincsar and Brown's notions rests upon the premise that children can be taught to internalize rules for comprehending over a period of time through the gradual removal of supportive scaffolds (Palincsar, 1984, 1986; Wood, Bruner, and Ross, 1976). This notion rests on the assumption that scaffolds are adjustable as well as temporary and that learning is a natural interactive process because it occurs in social contexts. It is highly dependent upon discussions between students and teachers. Alvermann, Dillon and O'Brien (1987) and Duffy and Roehler (1986) explain that discussion is a critical part of this type of teaching and learning because it is through discussion that the teacher learns what is in the students' minds, and thereby can restructure the situation to aid the student in understanding.

3 Understanding and Using Narrative Text Structure Knowledge Practices

Some researchers argue that explicit instruction of story structure is unnecessary because students will automatically acquire this knowledge indirectly as a byproduct of story listening/viewing (Moffett, 1983). Schmidt and O'Brien (1986) argued against instruction in narrative structure, suggesting that this form of instruction was both unnecessary and counterproductive; it emphasized only one piece of a story and deemphasized story content. However, there are other researchers who have found that instruction in narrative structure positively affects students' reading (McConaghy, 1980; Spiegel and Fitzgerald, 1986). Further, Buss, Ratliff, and Irion (1985) found that students who had little knowledge of story structure benefited considerably from direct instruction in story organization, specifically in story grammars.

4 Understanding and Using Expository Text Structure Knowledge Practices

Many researchers have reported that students at all grade levels can be taught the structures that underlie expository texts (Berkowitz,

1986; Taylor and Beach, 1984; Slater, Graves and Piche, 1985) and that the consistent use of this knowledge enhances recall and comprehension (Armbruster, Anderson and Ostertag, 1987; Baumann, 1984). Further, students who had the knowledge but did not use it were more negatively affected when reading texts with unfamiliar material than texts with familiar material (Meyer, Brandt, and Bluth, 1980; Taylor and Beach, 1984). At-risk students particularly benefit from instruction in text structure because it becomes a useful aid when the content is unfamiliar (Palincsar and Brown, 1985).

5   Questioning Practices: Question/Answer Relationships (QARs)

In several studies, Raphael (1982, 1986) demonstrated that students were capable of generating and answering questions that enhanced their comprehension and led to independent processing. She designed four types of QARs:

a. text-based QARs in which the answers are "right there," i.e., they are explicitly stated in the text;

b. text-based QARs in which the student has to "think and search" for relevant information throughout the text;

c. knowledge-based QARs in which the reader has to read the text to understand the question, but the answer is not in the text; and

d. knowledge-based QARs in which the student can answer the question without reading the text.

In the beginning stage of this process the teacher accepts total responsibility for the five key elements of the activity:

a. assigning the text,

b. generating the questions,

c. providing answers,

d. identifying the QAR, and

e. providing a justification for the QAR identified.

Eventually, control is released to the student after he or she has guided practice. In Raphael's studies, students who were trained in the QAR activity demonstrated significant gains in comprehension.

6 Inference Question Training Practices

Hansen and Hubbard (1984) tested a paradigm for inference training in which the teacher generated two questions—one to activate prior experience and one to generate predictions. Answers were shared in a group to expose students to many possible ideas. Students were able to answer the questions and to generate their own questions with novel texts.

7 Information Processing Practices

K-W-L: What We Know, What We Want to Find Out, What We Learn and Still Need to Learn.

The K-W-L procedure, developed by Ogle (1986), rests upon constructivist principles: it is the reader who ultimately must seek and find meaning. Initially, the student is shown how to use the guide. This is then followed by the teacher's question, "How do you know that?" which reminds the student to seek evidence from the text or from previous knowledge. This procedure is intended to activate, review, and develop background knowledge and to set useful purposes that will enable the student to be an independent learner.

Concept-Task-Application (C-T-A).

Wong and Au (1985) found that the asking of focused prereading discussion questions about critical concepts contained in the text enhanced students' background knowledge before reading. During this first (concept) phase, students set purposes for reading. The goal of the questions was twofold:

a. to find out what students already knew about a topic and

b. to determine what they still needed to know.

During the second stage, the task stage, the teacher asked cueing questions that focused the students' attention to important sections of the text, directing them to formulate satisfactory answers to the questions. When the students' answers indicated that comprehension was inaccurate or incomplete, the teacher asked questions that enabled the students to realize that they had a need for more information (which was frequently only available from an outside source) in order to "fix" their comprehension. The third stage, the application stage, occurred through a summarization process in which the teacher repeated the initial question and the student summarized all the information that had been discussed throughout the teaching/learning episode.

8 Developing Analogies Practices

Several researchers have demonstrated the effectiveness of using analogies to enhance comprehension (Hayes and Tierney, 1982; Peabody, 1984). Bean, Singer and Cowen (1985) developed an Analogical Study Guide to help students in biology understand the concepts that they were learning. In their study, they used the analogy of a functioning factory to understand the working of cells in the human body. Students who were given the analogical guide significantly outperformed students who were taught the information in more traditional ways.

9 Summarizing Practices

A renewed interest in summarization as a means for improving reading comprehension has occurred during the past few years. Much of this contemporary interest has been a result of Kintsch and Van Dijk's (1978) work that tied summarization ability to reading comprehension. The antecedents to this contemporary work can be found in a series of research studies conducted in the 1920s and 1930s. In 1934, after conducting several studies on summarizing, Salisbury found that students who were made aware of important points in the texts before reading and asked to summarize (list) the central ideas in the text had increased comprehension scores.

However, in its more recent development, summary writing has been difficult to describe because the summary itself has no universally accepted definition. Therefore, appropriate instruction that results in informal summaries is often very difficult to describe. However, even with that caveat, summary writing in its various forms still seems to be one of the best vehicles available for implementing a constructivist, process-oriented approach to teaching reading comprehension. Annis (1985) noted that the three traditionally accepted cognitive/linguistic requirements for comprehending prose form the basis for summary writing:

a. orientation of attention toward the task;

b. recording the information in the text into one's own words; and

c. making connections between the new material and one's prior knowledge.

As readers work through these three requirements, they are retelling the text. Retellings serve as a potent instructional technique for enhancing summarizing abilities as well as overall comprehension (Gambrell, Pfeiffer and Wilson, 1985).

10 Voluntary/Recreational Reading Practices

Several studies have indicated that few children or adults choose reading as a source of information or as a recreational activity (Anderson, Fielding and Wilson, 1985; Greaney and Hegarty, 1987; Morrow and Weinstein, 1982; Walberg and Tsai, 1984). Greaney's 1980 statistics on how many fifth graders read were alarming—almost one quarter of the students in his study said that they did no leisure reading. Conversely, several studies have revealed convincing data that suggest that students who engage in voluntary reading significantly outperform students who do not on all measures of comprehension (Long and Henderson, 1973; Irving, 1980; Morrow, 1983).

One contemporary approach to addressing the problems associated with aliterate students (those who can read but do not) has been the use of voluntary reading programs within and outside school. These programs forward the tenets of a constructivist approach to developing reading comprehension because they foster self-selection by the student, which in turn encourages personal meaning-making. When students select their own literature, they are taking a first step toward being responsible for their own comprehension development.

Several studies that examined the effectiveness of voluntary literature programs, in which classrooms were filled with high quality trade books, reported success in overall reading comprehension as well as improved attitudes toward reading (Ingham, 1981).

J. Estill Alexander
UNIVERSITY OF TENNESSEE, KNOXVILLE

1   Consider affective responses to learning as basic as cognitive responses.

2   Use "short term" skills groups when working on cognitive skills.

3   Foster lifelong reading interests.

4   Utilize diagnostic teaching procedures.

5   Build background (schemata) for new learning experiences.

6   Consider the impact of your (the teacher's) attitudes, nonverbal behavior, and modeling behaviors on students' learning.

7   Utilize ecologically valid assessment tools.

8   Teach students to use a variety of decoding strategies.

9   Develop and reinforce reading skills in content areas.

10 Utilize whole class, small group, and individualized instruction as appropriate to student and class needs.

Donna Alvermann

UNIVERSITY OF GEORGIA

1   Teach higher-order thinking strategies that use small-group discussion to integrate the four language arts: (reading, writing, listening, and speaking.

2   Select discussion strategies that activate or build background knowledge about the material to be read.

3   Emphasize discussion strategies that motivate students to examine the two sides of an issue in peer learning groups.

4   Give time for differing viewpoints, as well as consensus statements, to be shared during whole class discussion.

5   Instill within students the idea that a questioning attitude is a prerequisite for learning to read critically.

6   Remember that pseudo-discussions, or discussions in which rapid questioning and answering prevail, are not substitutes for discussions in which reflecting and elaborating occur.

7   Encourage students to direct their talk to each other, not just to the teacher or to the person facilitating the discussion.

8   Use questions for the purpose of clarifying and getting different points of view out in the open.

9   Remember that planning an effective post-reading discussion begins with determining its purpose; e.g., will it be for the purpose of learning specific content, for examining an issue, or for solving a problem?

10   Plan discussions that combine both small group and whole class interaction. Doing this will encourage each student to participate and yet allow time for large group synthesis as well.

Ernest Balajthy

STATE UNIVERSITY OF NEW YORK AT GENESEO

Too much computer-based instruction tempts us to forget that the children we teach are human beings that are in developmental process, not simply machines to be programmed. Here are some ideas for using computers in enriched, holistic ways that effectively convey to children that reading and writing are meaningful, communicative acts.

1 *Use guided language experience to help emergent readers through the transition from oral language to print.*

   - Programs such as *KidTalk* allow children to create their own stories on the computer.

   - *Explore-A-Story* combines reading children's story books (such as The *Lima Bean Dream*) with activities that extend reading through writing.

   - The *Language Experience Recorder* allows students to type their stories on disk and later print them out to make books.

2 *Follow the Whole Language movement in using highly predictable stories to enhance children's early reading.*

   For instance, *Student Stories* is a collection of predictable chant stories for use in emergent readers' choral reading or shared book lessons.

3 *Center classroom computer reading on interesting children's literature rather than dull basal stories.*

   The *Reading Comprehension Early Reading* series has stories from popular children's literature on each disk.

4 *Teach metacognitive skills using content area readings.*

   The *Comprehension Connection*, for example, helps middle-grade students develop their metacognitive "knowing that you know" skills.

5 *Provide feedback for writing during, not after, the writing process.*

   This message is central in the new writing process approaches to classroom writing instruction. Writing process curricula such as *Write Connection* and *Writing Workshop* provide prewriting, during-writing, and postwriting questions for students. *The Writing Notebook* (P.O. Box 79, Mendocino, CA 95460) is a quarterly magazine that has a wealth of creative, writing process ideas for using word processors and other writing software in the classroom.

6   *Let children choose their own books and spend in-class time in sustained silent reading.*

BookBrain administers a quick interest survey, then provides an annotated bibliography of suggested books to the student.

7   *Use computers as an integral part of thematic units that integrate varied aspects of the total curriculum.*

In a unit on The Westward Expansion, for instance, many computer-based language activities can be incorporated. Students can create party invitations for a frontier-style class party, banners to advertise important historical events, and posters about famous people using newer, improved printing programs such as *Print Magic.* Students can make crossword puzzles of important vocabulary words using *Crossword Magic.* They can create a graphic timeline paralleling events on the American western frontier with events in Europe and Asia using *Time Liner.* Simulation games such as *Oregon Trail* can provide them with some of the experiences of living on the frontier.

8   *Have students publish to develop a sense of authorship.*

One local remedial reading class uses a classroom desktop publishing program to publish a newsletter for the parents of the children.

9   *Help students recognize that learning is a social event by structuring cooperative learning environments.*

Research indicates that cooperative learning, appropriately managed, is superior to competitive learning. The amount of student cooperation in classroom learning tasks seems to increase almost automatically when computers are introduced into the language classroom.

10 *Stay abreast of professional developments in using computers to teaching reading and writing by reading* Micro Missive, *the quarterly newsletter of the International Reading Association's Special Interest Group for Microcomputers in Reading.*

Contact Dr. Kent Layton, Arkansas State University, Department of Elementary Education, State University, AR 72467 for information.

References

Bookbrain. (Phoenix, Ariz.: Oryx Press, 1988)

Comprehension Connection. (St. Louis, Mo: Milliken, 1987)

Crossword Magic. (Glenview, Ill.: Scott Foresman, 1985)

Explore-a-Story. (Lexington, Mass.: D.C. Heath, 1987)

KidTalk. (Long Beach, Calif.: First Byte, 1986)

Language Experience Recorder. (Gainesville, Fla.: Teacher Support Software, 1986)

Oregon Trail. (St. Paul, Minn.: Minnesota Educational Computing Corporation, 1983)

Print Magic. (Redwood City, Calif.: Epyx, 1987)

Reading Comprehension Early Reading. (Hanover, N.H.: Houghton Mifflin Educational Software, 1988)

Student Stories. (St. Paul, Minn.: Minnesota Educational Computing Corporation, 1985)

Time Liner. (Cambridge, Mass.: Tom Snyder Productions, 1987)

Write Connection. (Glenview, Ill.: Scott Foresman, 1989)

Writing Workshop. (St. Louis, Mo.: Milliken, 1985)

Richard Bamberger

INSTITUTE FOR SCHOOLBOOK RESEARCH, VIENNA, AUSTRIA

1 *Try to secure as much time as possible for reading.*

Steal it from other subjects (they get a lot more in return). Steal it from television time.

2 *Start your lessons where your students are.*

Keep in mind their reading capacity, their interests, and their aims. (Most children prefer exciting stories or books; some seem to like factual material better.)

3 *Lure students into reading by telling them an exciting or interesting story or—still better—part of a book.*

In this way you hook them with the action, the exciting plot. The children read further in the class and finish the book at home within one or two days.

4 *Introduce a reader's passport with pages for different purposes:*

- results of achievement tests,
- a survey of books read with marks denoting how children liked each book,
- a list of recommended books that have bearing to the test results.

5 *Don't waste time developing reading skills by using special exercises, but rely on the amount of reading material or the time spent for reading.*

6 *Forget the communication aspect.*

Students should talk less about what they have read and instead use the time for reading more.

7 *Use reading material that leads children on to related topics or books, thereby introducing new material.*

8 *Combine reading and writing activities by having children complete stories that have been read to them in part.*

We have "write-on books" in our classes, where the best endings are collected. These stories are used as reading material in class.

9 *Note*: Many children do not read books because they cannot read (properly); they cannot read because they do not read books.

10 *Note*: Many children do not read because they could not tackle the first two or three stories or picture books they were given to read.

(PERSONAL OPINION OF AN EDITOR)

Janet Binkley

INTERNATIONAL READING ASSOCIATION

I have one idea that's as important as any ten others for reading teachers—for any teachers, really. It didn't come out of my years of teaching, however, but out of the years I've spent in business and publishing, in the world of modern work for which schools are ultimately preparing children:

Teachers need to prepare young people to work cooperatively, in teams, on shared projects.

In schools children are isolated, actually taught not to help each other either to plan or carry out their tasks. As adults, though, most of us work constantly in cooperation with others. Our individual task is just one node in a mesh that changes from day to day. What we do, and how and when we do it, are all determined by the current progress of the larger project and the related tasks of our fellow workers.

Learning to work in tandem with others doesn't happen overnight, and it doesn't happen much in American schools. It's often the most difficult adjustment and learning task for young people in their first full-time job. Yet it needn't be; there's no reason schools can't structure learning projects as cooperative ones.

For many teachers, there's a hard spot in this—namely, they feel obliged to give students a grade for every learning task. For the sake of grades, teachers may unintentionally undermine the goal of teaching young people to be willing, knowledgeable, cheerful cooperators, as most of us must be in our adult work lives.

For example, I've seen teachers give individual grades based on the overall quality of a small group's final product. While this may at first glance seem reasonable, it shifts the group's focus away from their cooperative effort and from the learning involved in the task (which are the teacher's intent) and onto the final grade. Group grades are also a turnoff for the best students, who resent the danger of having their grade averages lowered.

The teacher can avoid these problems by rating not the group product but the learning that took place. For example, you can set the class a project doing library research and developing a group paper on a topic. Then, rather than grading the final papers the various small groups develop, you can give a quiz over the topic area and grade each student for what that person learned during the research and writing.

This parallels what happens in the world of work. Projects require the work of many people, but some individuals are seen to be more productive and learn more, and they move up the organization into more demanding positions.

Another alternative in schools is to give up the idea of grading everything students do. Give them an interesting, substantive project, in groups, and let that task pass without a grade. Make it a pass/rework situation, requiring a certain standard of product for acceptance as completed. Again, that's the way the business world operates, so it's good training for students of any age.

In the last ten years, there's been plenty of research on cooperative learning. It shows that students learn better and like school better—and like each other better!—when major learning tasks are structured cooperatively. For starters, see the research reported by Roger and David Johnson, brothers at the University of Minnesota.

Still there's been little change in this direction in most classrooms. I think teachers find it hard to set up cooperative projects except when it's something for "fun and games." We didn't grow up with them ourselves, so we're not sure how to go about it. Also, we distrust them. Maybe we've been brainwashed to believe that competition is the only way things get achieved, so we don't believe the research on students' progress in cooperative learning when we read it.

Still I believe that even if students didn't learn history or geography or science better through cooperative projects, they need to acquire the feeling that working with other people is natural and comfortable and productive, because that's how they're going to spend their adult lives. The fact that individual learning actually goes on better in small groups is just one super extra benefit for reading teachers.

Ronald P. Carver

UNIVERSITY OF MISSOURI AT KANSAS CITY

1   Encourage children to read books.

2   Help children learn to enjoy reading.

3   See that children read at least one library book each week.

4   Make sure that all children have access to books that they find both easy and interesting.

5   Help children find books to read that are at their own reading level.

6   Avoid asking children to read books that are too difficult for them, because they are likely to become frustrated with reading.

7   Read books aloud to children that are at their auditory level of ability, which is usually higher than their reading level.

8   Find books that are tape recorded so that children can read along as they listen to their own book.

9   Don't spend a lot of time on work sheets and skill sheets related to reading; more than 15 minutes a day is too much.

10 Encourage children to read books.

Alan N. Crawford

CALIFORNIA STATE UNIVERSITY, LOS ANGELES

1   Students only learn to read once; the skills they develop in one language will positively transfer to another. Bilingual education is what we call that process of positive transfer of skills.

2   Language-minority students from lower socioeconomic circumstances who are moving from a language of low prestige (for them) to a language of higher prestige (for them) will ordinarily learn to read more effectively in their primary language than in their second language.

3   The stronger the base of students' primary languages, the more rapidly and effectively they will acquire a second or third language, including mastery of its reading and writing processes.

4   It is probably more important to provide a core literature/integrated language arts/whole language approach to language minority students, who often have reading and writing problems, than to "successful" middle-class students. Often the middle-class students are viewed as those best able to benefit from an integrated approach because they can already read and write well, and the skills-based approach is reserved for minority students because they lack skills.

5   The readiness of a student in primary language reading to make the transition to reading in the English language should depend more on the student's ability to deal with connected discourse (oral or written) than on skill development in either the primary or second language.

6   Despite the regularity of phoneme-grapheme relationships in the Spanish language, most Spanish-speaking nations use a global or global structural-analytic approach to the teaching of reading. Is there a lesson to be learned here in a nation whose language has largely irregular phoneme-grapheme relationships and which often attempts to impose a phonetic approach to reading instruction, not only on its own native English speakers, but also on students who may lack fully one third of the sounds of the English language in their repertoire?

7   Infants don't seem to have any problems learning their mother tongue. We need to replicate in the classroom the home environment that facilitates that language acquisition process—language input that is comprehensible and contextual, a silent period, a low anxiety level, and a lack of correction. Incomplete or incorrect utterances should be viewed as immature, not incorrect.

8   As a beginning strategy, the language experience approach is still the most powerful approach to reading instruction because it most clearly relates oral language to the written word.

9   It is more important for language minority students than for other students that they not study about reading and writing—they should rather read and write about the real things they are studying.

10   Reading is a synergistic process; the whole is greater than the sum of the parts.

Patricia M. Cunningham

WAKE FOREST UNIVERSITY

James W. Cunningham

UNC, CHAPEL HILL

(The scene opens in a log house in Gibsonville, North Carolina. It is a Monday evening around eight o'clock when Jim returns from Chapel Hill and asks his usual question.)

Jim: Anything interesting in the mail?

Pat: You won't believe this, but there actually was something interesting today. What would you say if someone asked you what the ten greatest ideas in reading were?

Jim: Well, instructional level for sure and then there's language experience, sustained silent reading...

(Jim continues to reel off great ideas. Pat looks on in amazement.)

Pat: I can't believe you can just do that. Don't you even want to know why I asked or who wants to know?

Jim: Well, sure, but you did ask. Who wants to know?

(Pat hands Jim Ed Fry's letter explaining about the conferences and the book in memory of Harry.)

Jim: This is a really clever idea—Harry would have loved it. It is exactly the kind of thing he would have done!

Pat: Good, then we'll write it. It isn't due 'til June first.

(Scene Two takes place in late May at The Jefferson House over barbecue, cornbread, fried squash, pinto beans, and iced tea.)

Jim: I just don't know about this task. The more I think about it the more impossible it seems. How narrow or broad should a "great idea" be? Are there really eight or thirteen? Pass the barbecue sauce, please.

Pat: Well, we really have to write this thing. I suggest we make a list of all the possibilities, then try to pick the ten best.

(Jim nods agreement and Pat takes out a yellow legal pad and begins to write as they brainstorm great ideas:

- instructional level

- reading/writing connections

- prediction

- DR-TA

- language experience

- phonemic segmentation

- every-pupil response activities

- spelling approaches to decoding

(At one point they get off task and begin listing the worst ideas: Words in Color, Tach X, Frostig. . . This is a lot more fun but not very productive! The final list of candidates for the top ten has 32 items. Then the elimination begins. Time passes.)

Pat: Well, we've got six for sure and nine others. Maybe there are only six great ideas and the other four have yet to be discovered. Why don't we just do six?

Jim: Because ten is the magic number. Dick Clark counted down the top ten. Bestsellers come in tens. Harry always did ten. We have to have ten!

Pat: Well, I think ten is arbitrary! But, Ed did say ten. Let's talk about the six we are sure about and why we are so sure about those and then maybe we will be able to narrow the rest down some more.

Waitress, could we please have some more tea?

1 Instructional Level

The concept of instructional level is critical because some books are much harder to read than others. What makes material difficult or easy includes such diverse components as sight word knowledge, decoding ability, prior knowledge, interest, and motivation. Measuring instructional level is not an exact science. There is no standardized test that can do it. Readability formulas often mislabel the true difficulty of text. The best way to determine instructional level remains some version of the old IRI. An informal reading inventory, as originally devised, was a tryout with the actual materials to be used. Teachers took the books available for instruction and had children read aloud and respond to questions about what they read. Of course, today's teacher should probably be trained to use diagnosis by observation to evaluate the appropriateness of the match between book and student rather than the time-consuming individual testing of yesteryear. Maybe Book Tryouts are a better term than IRI.

A book tryout is analagous to going to the store to try on shoes. Different styles and makes vary and the clerk makes a beginning guess based on the shoe gauge and then the shoe buyer "tries them out" under the watchful eye and probing questioning of the clerk. (Are they slipping? How does the left one feel in front?) Sometimes when you get them home, the shoes still don't work out and have to be changed or scrapped, but shoes bought after careful tryouts have a much better chance of giving a comfortable fit than shoes bought just by size.

"Instructional level" is kind of an old-fashioned term. Nowadays, it is more fashionable to talk about "daily success." Whatever it is called, some books are a lot harder than others, and if children are to grow in reading, they must be given instruction in books that allow them to be successful at figuring out most of the words and understanding most of what they read. Certainly those students who are going to be good readers have been given materials with which they are highly successful in both oral and silent reading.

2 Language Experience

Language experience is critical for young readers and writers because it lets them see inside the process. It is hard for us who have been literate for such a long time to realize what a totally arbitrary and abstract process written communication is. There are so many things to be learned, from the big idea that "writing is talk written down" to the small but critical print conventions. Our eyes must move all the way across the line left to right, and then rather than work our way back right to left (which does seem as if it would save time!), we must make a return sweep and start again. The little tiny space (which does not exist between spoken words) signals the end of one word and the beginning of another. Even the concept of word is a mystery until you confront and understand the arbitrary working of written language.

Language experience occurs when Mom records a dictated "thank you" letter to Grandma. Language experience occurs when the toddler is helping to make the grocery list by calling out items needed and watching as they are written down. Language experience is one way children get both the big picture and the minute, critical details of written language. Language experience is also one of the original forms of the currently "in" modeling process.

3 Reading/Writing Connections

The current practice of connecting reading and writing experiences has come in and out of fashion but is clearly one of the great ideas. In recent U.S. reading history, children were taught to read first. Only when they could read and spell and correctly form the letters in upper and lower case, were they allowed to write. By then, many children had decided writing was a slow, onerous, rule-governed process. Contrast this with beginning literacy practices in many countries of the world in which children are encouraged to write from the first day of school. At first they draw and scribble. As their notions of words and letters grow, they incorporate these notions into their writing. Writing in much of the world is an active, child-centered entry into literacy.

Currently, early writing is beginning to be encouraged in this country. We are seeing that children who are allowed to write not only become better writers, they become better readers. As they try to spell words, they apply whatever letter-sound relationships they are learning. Word walls or personal dictionaries of commonly used words helps children learn to read the high-frequency words they write often. As children mature as writers, they come to understand that everything they read has an author who, like them, is trying to communicate something. Writers who begin to read like writers become much more critical and appreciative readers. Readers who are also writers try out various writing techniques they have encountered in their own reading. Connecting reading and writing from the very beginning and onward throughout schooling is a win-win proposition.

4 Sustained Silent Reading

The idea that the goal of reading instruction is reading is still one of the truest ideas of all times. The problem has been how to implement that goal in the heavily scheduled school day of the average teacher and class. Sustained silent reading was a great idea because it made it possible to have real reading going on in real classrooms. Sustained silent reading has as its critical components the notions of reader choice of material, time to read, no reports or other "extrinsic" motivation for reading, and the need for any adults present to demonstrate the importance of reading by reading also. Currently the term is out of fashion, but the ideas are embodied in such notions as "literature-based reading programs," "voluntary reading," and "recreational reading."

5 Schema Theory

Schema theory's contribution is that the reader is brought back into the reading process. Schema theory research demonstrates for all time that reading is an interaction between what is on the page and what is in the mind of the reader, and that often what is in the reader's head overrides what is on the page. Readers don't bring a blank page to the book page. Rather, they bring a network of prior knowledge, preconceptions, purposes, and motivations that determine what and how much they understand and remember. When prior knowledge is severely limited, comprehension is seriously impaired. When preconceptions are actually misconceptions, these misconceptions are often maintained in spite of the counter evidence provided in the reading.

Schema theory reminds us that the act of reading—like many other important parts of life—has a before, a during, and an after. Before reading, readers must get their schemas out. During reading they confirm, change and add to these schemas. After reading, they consolidate and accommodate. Prior knowledge affects what is taken to reading, what is obtained from reading, and what is changed as a result of reading.

Moreover, schema theory makes us realize that a skills-based or strategy-based curriculum dooms many children to illiteracy. Without knowledge, skills and strategies either will not be learned or will not be applied during reading and writing. Teaching science, social studies, health, art, and music well supports literacy rather than competes with it! We used to say that every teacher is a teacher of reading. Now we know that every teacher should be a teacher of knowledge.

6   Reading Recovery

Reading recovery is only six years old in the U.S., but it has been a part of the New Zealand system for over a decade. Reading recovery in action can be seen at the parent site, Ohio State University in Columbus, and at spinoff sites around the country. Trained reading recovery teachers work with first graders from the bottom 20% of the class on an individual basis. They have books carefully divided into 24 levels based on tryouts with hundreds of reading recovery children. (Notice again the importance of instructional level!) After ten days of "roaming the known," the teacher places the child in the correct level of books. The child then reads many books in that level. During each thirty-minute session, the child reads at least three books, writes, and is given guidance in letter-sound relationships based on the actual texts read and written. There is no isolated drill or practice.

Reading recovery is in demand everywhere because it has the data to show that it works. Over 80 percent of reading recovery children read on grade level when they exit the program and they are still on grade level at the end of third grade. Reading recovery may be the greatest idea of this century. It is certainly the greatest idea of this decade.

(Scene three takes place on May 24 around the Mac in the log house.)

Pat: Well, here we are again—down to the wire on this dumb thing. I don't know why we ever agreed to this.

Jim: We still have a week before it's due! I don't know why you're panicking.

Pat: You know I hate doing things at the last minute. Now, we either have to send it in with six or we have to decide on four more. Maybe we should put our remaining ones in a hat and just draw four.

Jim: (pretending he didn't hear this suggestion) Well, I still think we should include:

7 Graphic Organizers

Graphic organizers forced us to understand the importance of text structure and focused everyone's attention on text structure. It was one thing to harangue publishers about "considerate text" and something else again when teachers and students began making webs, outlines, timelines, feature matrices, data charts and other devices which graphically depict the organization of the text ideas. Once students and teachers actually started to organize the text, they discovered that some textbook text wouldn't graphically organize! Students were presented with one fact after another with no structure. The definition of inconsiderate text became almost synonymous with text that couldn't be graphically organized. Writers and textbook publishers began to apply this criterion to their text and the result is better written textbooks. When students learn to make graphic organizers, they become aware of how important understanding relationships is to learning and remembering information. When the relationships are not readily apparent, they ask themselves, "How can I organize this information?" When repeated attempts to graphically depict relationships fail, students and teachers realize that their comprehension problems are partly a result of inconsiderate text and they demand better organized reading material.

Graphic organizers are also a great idea for supporting the notions of schema theory in the classroom. In fact, graphic organizers were probably first used to show the relationships between meaning vocabulary in a text or unit of study. And graphic organizers have been used in a variety of reading comprehension and writing lesson frameworks to communicate the concept of interrelationships of ideas to students without having to use a lot of jargon.

8 Automaticity

Automaticity was a great idea because it marked the beginning of our shift away from a "one skill at a time" mentality towards a "reading is a juggling act" conceptualization. The notion that we had limited attention, and that anything that took part of that attention left less to allocate to other functions seems obvious now but was not obvious in the way we taught reading in the early seventies. Automaticity explains why students could read sight words on flash cards but not read those same words in connected text. Automaticity explains the common teachers' complaint that "students know the skills, they just don't use them." Automaticity has also made rereading a text an acceptable and valued part of reading instruction.

Pat: Okay, you've convinced me. We still need two more and I am going to go out on a limb and include:

9 Integrated Curriculum

Integrated curriculum was known in the old days as "the unit approach to teaching." Integrated curriculum is much more encompassing than "language arts integration" and is more balanced than "content area reading" (both among the candidates for these two remaining spots). Integrated curriculum means that all learning is purposeful. The starting is usually some content area topic—weather, Australia, reproduction. Learning about this topic drives the skills and strategies (in the broadest sense) students employ. They find information in textbooks and locate other sources of information. They research, read, write, listen, speak, act—perhaps even sing and dance! Even mathematics is included in truly integrated units as students solve problems which involve numbers. Integration can even cut across science, social studies, and health lines, since most important topics have implications for all three subject areas. Often art, music, and literature find a place in the integration, too.

Integrated curriculum has always been more a great idea in theory than in practice. Textbooks are produced by separate divisions in publishing companies. States adopt by subject area in different cycles. Teachers and students are often "departmentalized." Report cards have separate grades for the separate subjects. Schools often contain music, art, physical education, science, and reading "specialists."

Because integrated curriculum has so many barriers to implementation, we have fought including it. But it is clearly one of the great ideas for reading because reading in real life is seldom divorced from interest in a topic. While totally integrated curriculum can probably never be achieved, it is a great idea worth striving for.

Jim: Well, one more and I have it. The final great idea is:

10 Great Ideas

Many brilliant and caring people have applied their energies to the study and teaching of reading down through the decades. As a result, there have been many ideas in the form of materials, teaching strategies, tests, principles, and insights. Of course, some of these have been discarded as they have been found to be less than great. (We will again resist the temptation to list our worst ten.) Fortunately, there has been an accumulation of good ideas that each decade of reading people, including our own, has attempted to add to. We have listed only ten, but there have been many more. The only times that the field of reading seems to be generally ineffective is when there is a mass movement to ignore the great ideas, either by a primitivism which would have us return to some "golden age," or a modernism which would have us discard all we have learned for some new panacea or revolution. Literacy will only approach universality when schools implement a large set of great ideas.

Pat: I guess I'm pretty satisfied with our ten, although there are a couple of others I would like to have included. How about you?

Jim: Yes, except I can't wait to see what the next great idea will be!

Dan Donlan

UNIVERSITY OF CALIFORNIA, RIVERSIDE

As a former high school English and reading teacher, I had to go back quite a way for my ten best ideas. All ten are language-based activities that I used to motivate students to read certain literary and nonliterary texts.

1 Where Language Began

Have your students put themselves in the place of cavemen who wish to leave some message on the walls for the next cave dwellers. Have each student "write" her or his autobiography without using language—in other words, by confining the effort to pictures. Have the students exchange and translate the pictures into standard English. When the translations are returned to their original owners, the discrepancies in communication can be discussed.

2 The Development of Language

Whisper a nonsense word into the ear of the first student in the first row. Write down what you said, but keep it concealed from the students. The first student whispers the word into the ear of the student in back of him or her. The first student then writes down what he or she whispered to the second student. The process is repeated until the word has gone around the room. Compare the final written version with the original written version. Trace how the word "developed" as it was passed around the room, by recording the individual written variations on the blackboard. Show the students a chart indicating the Indo-European language family. Tell them that the same word-of-mouth transfer of language produced as many language variations as were produced within the classroom.

3 Invent a Word

Have students invent objects, using materials close at hand, such as paper, tape, pins, and chalk. With the students, give the objects names. Translate the names into written symbols, or words. Next ask students to describe the objects in sentences.

4 Manufacturing a Word

Prepare a list of common prefixes, stems, and suffixes. Instruct students to invent a word, building it from one prefix, one stem, and one suffix. Have students write their words on the bottom of a piece of construction paper, then illustrate the word with a magazine collage and define it. Students may include diacritical marks, if they wish. The word is then to be used in a sentence with contextual clues.

5 Working with Dictionaries

Before you begin this activity, check with your librarian to make sure that all the dictionaries described in the following activities are available and that they may be used in your classroom. Divide your class of students into three groups of equal size. Supply each group with a different dictionary, such as *The Shorter Oxford English Dictionary, Part I; The Shorter Oxford English Dictionary, Part II*; and *The Dictionary of Contemporary American Usage*. Each group will work with a dictionary for fifteen minutes, then rotate the dictionary to the next group for fifteen minutes, then rotate again for another fifteen minutes. By the end of the period, each group should have completed an assignment in each of the three dictionaries. Appoint one person in each group to be in charge of looking up the words or expressions in the dictionary and reading the information to the rest of the group. The group participants are to copy the information in their notebooks. One volunteer should make a copy for the group leader.

6 Teaching Spelling

Spelling is one of the most frustrating problems in teaching. Students who receive high scores on spelling quizzes seem to misspell the same words when they write, even seconds after the quiz. There seems to be a correlation between how much a student reads and how well he spells, which might lead one to assume that problem readers could never be taught to spell. However, some problem readers are good spellers and some competent readers are poor spellers. Since students don't seem to learn spelling words from lists, teaching a context for spelling is more effective. I always advocated a weekly list of words based around a theme or topic for the week.

This list would include words used frequently in class discussions and in writing activities over a period of a week. Words could even be drawn from what the students are reading.

7   Semantics and the Feeling Tone of Words

Here is an exercise that makes students think about language choices.

Instructions:

Tact is an important part of maintaining good human relations. Rewrite the following statements tactfully.

a. Mr. Jones, you're fired.

b. Mary, we voted you out of the club yesterday.

c. Jerry, I decided not to go with you anymore. Here is your engagement ring.

d. I'm not going to school, and there's nothing you can do to make me.

e. I ran over your dog and killed it.

8   Semantics, Compliments and Insults

Students should be taught that word choice is important in expressing a specific emotion or attitude. For example, you can call someone a "scholar" or an "egg-head." Students can have fun with this exercise:

Instructions:

Arrange each set of the following words from positive to negative: for example, *angel, child, brat, monster.*

a. smart, brainy, smart-aleck, intelligent, pseudo-intellectual, brilliant

b. verbose, fluent, verbal, talkative, loud-mouthed, loquacious

c. demanding, strict, tough, unyielding, rigorous, narrow-minded

9   Making Sense from Nonsense

Have your students read Lewis Carroll's "Jabberwocky" and substitute words they know for the nonsense words, making sure that the entire rewritten poem makes sense.

10 Free Association to Music

Have the students divide a sheet of paper into fourths horizontally. Play four recorded selections of mood music, preferably contrasting moods, and have students write down whatever comes into their minds as they are listening to each selection. No writing is to be done between selections. After the music is finished, discuss what moods the music suggested. Students will notice how the emotional tone of their writing has changed with the changes in music. Also, discuss with them the value of studying with music as a background.

Mariam Jean Dreher

UNIVERSITY OF MARYLAND, COLLEGE PARK

1   Whatever the grade level, read to your students from good literature every day.

2   Allocate time every day for students to read from books they enjoy.

3   Teach students the process of active comprehension by having them learn to formulate their own questions before, during, and after reading. Part of teaching students to be active comprehenders involves having teachers learn to ask questions that elicit questions rather than answers (Singer, 1978; Singer and Donlan, 1989).

4   To help motivate disabled readers, use a cumulative graph to document their progress. The number of pages a student reads at each session is graphed. However, the pages for each session start where the last session page numbers left off. With a progress record that starts at zero for each session, students eventually reach a point where they can't outdo the previous session's performance unless the sessions become ever lengthier. Moreover, a cumulative graph can go up or stay level, but it can't go down—even if a student backslides. Such a graph, as shown in Figure 1, gives visible evidence of effort and puts learning under the student's control (Singer and Beasley, 1970).

Figure 1

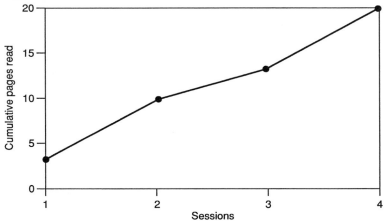

5   When planning reading lessons for poor readers, think about what you would do with younger good readers who were reading at that level (Richard Allington at a presentation in Maryland, about 1981).

6   When evaluating instructional strategies, look beyond the surface manifestations. Try to determine what cognitive processes the strategy helps students engage in. It is these cognitive processes that make the difference (Tobias, 1982).

7   Create independent learners by using the phase in/phase out technique as you teach each new process or strategy. This technique consists of phasing in the students as you phase out the teacher. Begin by modeling the strategy and working through it with the entire group. Then have students practice in subgroups and finally engage in the strategy independently (Singer and Donlan, 1989).

Priscilla A. Drum

University of California, Santa Barbara

1 Read the best materials you can find to nonreaders. Include many informative pieces.

2 Learning how to read entails learning how to match visual signs to speech sounds. The key word here is *how*. The ultimate goal of reading is to obtain the meaning contained in the visual message. Before this can be accomplished, however, primary learning involves the recognition and match of visual symbols to speech units.

3 Both speed and accuracy in word recognition are necessary. The mental manipulation of ideas cannot occur until the word recognition skills are fairly facile.

4 Practice reading is the best means for developing fluency in word recognition. Emerging readers should be given practice time in which they silently read different texts that are easily within their understanding. Rereading the same book also develops fluency in word recognition.

5 Understanding what is read is limited by language knowledge. Do not expect most new readers to obtain meaning from texts that they cannot comprehend orally.

6 New concepts need to be taught prior to reading about them. Do not expect most novices to learn material via reading alone.

7 Content area vocabulary provides a structured overview for any introductory topic. Novice learners need help in building up a conceptual structure using the vocabulary of that subject.

8 Knowing the organization of a text aids both comprehension and retention. "Event texts" like newspaper articles and bibliographies often use a "who, what, why, when, where, how" organization. Nonevent texts often use combinations of compare/contrast, major ideas and supporting details/examples/illustrations, and so on. Aspiring readers are aided in both comprehending and retaining

information if they understand the organizational structures for texts.

9   Active comprehension participation helps learning if the techniques fit the specific material. Study skills approaches, such as survey, question, read, recite, and review; comprehension monitoring; or predicting ahead while reading are all based on the premise of active participation.

10   Appropriate text selection depends upon the knowledge of the prospective readers and the goals for reading. If the text contains nothing but common knowledge that is already known by the prospective readers, then the text is too simple for new learning. If the information contains too much new (unknown) material, then many readers will be unable to comprehend it and give up. What is the appropriate ratio of new versus old information? These are mainly judgment calls by those selecting texts. Perhaps the best solution is to make multiple texts on a topic available so that each text can reinforce the others, add additional information, or provide alternate explanations.

Thomas H. Estes

UNIVERSITY OF VIRGINIA

1 Prior knowledge is the most important factor influencing new learning. Teach from what students already know to what you want them to learn.

2 Students will learn more from activities in which they are actively engaged than from activities they merely do to get done.

3 Teach up. You'll often get performance from students at a higher level than you have any reason to think possible.

4 The best questions to ask are those to which there is not one right answer.

5 Vocabulary and conceptual development are essentially related; knowledge of vocabulary reflects a stage of understanding.

6 Give students multiple opportunities to learn the same thing, multiple sources to learn from. Real reading is always done in a context of learning and is rarely limited to a single source.

7 People learn to read by practicing reading.

8 Disciplines of knowledge are interconnected and they are best taught in ways that make their connections apparent.

9 The most important thing students have to learn is how to learn, how to construct understandings. Fortunately, the proper framework for teaching and a constructivist framework of learning are congruent. Teaching and learning proceed in three phases: anticipations (based on prior knowledge), realizations (based on connections perceived in knowledge), and contemplations (based on the complementary processes of assimilation and accommodation).

10 The law of meaningful processing holds—other things being equal, people learn and remember more when conditions require them to understand the material. This is the basis of the Directed Reading-Thinking Activity first proposed by Stauffer (1969) and still the best general lesson plan for teaching reading.

Yetta M. Goodman and Kenneth S. Goodman

University of Arizona

1 Miscues reflect intellectual functioning and knowledge on the part of the reader.

Our research into reading, writing and oral language processes has shown that miscues (originally developed as a concept by Kenneth Goodman in reading research), occur in all language use and language learning. Analysis of miscues has provided evidence of the universal reading strategies of predicting, inferencing, and confirming involved in the construction of meaning. Miscues during reading and retellings reflect both the conceptual and linguistic knowledge that readers bring to the reading process and show the influence of prior knowledge on the reading process. The concept of invented spelling is related to the concept of miscues. Children's invented spellings show that language users are involved in the invention of all aspects of language use. Invented spelling also reveals a reader or writer's knowledge of all the language cueing systems.

Through the miscues and invented spellings produced by readers and writers, researchers and teachers build insights into how the reading and writing processes work and the degree to which readers are willing to take risks as they read.

2 Readers and writers develop best when they are willing to take risks.

The confidence that readers and writers bring to their reading and writing influences their development. This relates to the concept of risk taking. Predicting, confirming, and making inferences about what is being read and preplanning, composing, and revising during writing are all related to taking personal responsibility for constructing meaning. Readers and writers must believe that they know enough to create meaning. If learners do not believe in the worthiness of their knowledge, then they may see no reasons to access their prior knowledge in order to construct meanings. Learners must feel comfortable to guess, to experiment with, and to be tentative about their growing meanings. These reading and writing strategies are all predicated on risk-taking abilities.

3   *Teaching and learning are not one-to-one isomorphic relationships.*

For too long instruction, especially in the field of reading, has reflected the view that the particular knowledge a teacher is teaching at a particular moment should be immediately learned by the reader. Tests and lessons are designed to prove that students have learned what has just been taught. As a result, the focus in educational research has been to discover a single best teaching methodology. The work of scholars such as Piaget and Vygotsky, among others, has demonstrated that learners are active participants in their learning and that learning is a complex and continuous activity, not something activated only when a teacher is directly teaching a specific skill or strategy.

Teaching is not simply the presentation of knowledge. Rather it involves planning for and organizing an environment that invites readers to find reason and purpose to want to read. Many would suggest that teachers who develop such an environment are not teaching, and therefore do not play an important role in students' learning to read. Nothing is farther from the truth. Learning to read and write are processes that individuals develop. Such processes can be supported and developed better in certain settings than in others. It is necessary to understand how much teaching supports readers' development.

4   *Decisions learners make about joining the literacy club explain why some students learn to read easily and others have much more difficulty.*

The concept of the literacy club, popularized by Frank Smith, places literacy learning in the larger cultural context where it belongs. It focuses away from the notion that a specific methodology is responsible for the teaching of reading. Rather the concept of the literacy club suggests that there are many forces in society that influence learning to read. These influences may help the learner relate to those in society who believe that literacy learning is important or may convince the learner that the dues that are necessary to become part of that club are too dear to pay for admission.

It is incumbent on teachers and developers of reading instruction to be consciously aware of the literacy club metaphor and organize for social settings and experiences in which students feel comfortable to take the necessary risks to build their literacy.

5 Understanding the concept of the zone of proximal development enhances the learning process.

Vygotsky's concept of the zone of proximal development is reminiscent of the folk saying, "Two heads are better than one." The zone of proximal development simply means that a learner can learn better with the supportive help of others. It legitimatizes the popularity of collaborative and cooperative learning.

The way in which the zone is organized is crucial. A teacher can organize for a zone of proximal development by setting up opportunities for the learner to work with the teacher, other adults, or peers. In such supportive relationships students work beyond what they do by themselves. Schools and classrooms need to be organized to capitalize on collaborations and the support of the learning community. Serious consideration of the social nature of schooling in support of the zone of proximal development will encourage membership in the literacy club. On the other hand the school/classroom environment can be set up in such a way so that there is a gatekeeping effect; the zone of proximal development is not activated; and learners begin to believe that they are not an integral part of the social community of the classroom and therefore not invited to join the literacy club.

6 What is being learned must be tied to what is already known.

The concept of schema, well developed by Piaget, suggests the importance of the knowledge base readers have. Knowledge and understandings are expanded as readers build on the understandings they already possess.

Teachers must respect the knowledge that readers have, help readers have confidence in what they already know, and legitimatize the importance of what they know. In this way students are more likely to access their prior knowledge and recognize that what they are learning is related to other events and experiences in their lives.

7 Exploring a personal model of the reading/learning process aids in teaching and learning.

Views of reading and learning influence how people read and learn. The ways in which teachers construct reading instruction, publishers organize reading and instructional materials, and authors write for readers are all governed by their own views of the reading and learning processes. These messages often have great influence on the views that students develop of the reading process and the degree to which they come to believe they have control over the reading process.

8 Kidwatching provides a powerful way for teachers to evaluate readers' progress as well as their own teaching.

Kidwatching suggests that teachers are interpreting the nature of the students' reading and the value of the knowledge they are developing in every transaction they have with their students. Kidwatching is a concept of placing evaluation of students in the hands of a professional educator and helping educators become comfortable with their responsibilities as evaluators. Teachers need to be knowledgeable about language (including the reading process), language learning, teaching, and curriculum in order to know what their observations mean in relation to the growth and development of students' reading.

9 Reflective thinking provides a powerful process for learning.

John Dewey's discussion of reflective thinking reveals the process of self evaluation on the part of both the teacher and the student. The greatest form of evaluation is the ability of teachers and students to think critically about what they are doing, why they are doing it, what significance what they are doing has for language use and language learning, and to make the necessary changes in their lives to accommodate their self critique. Like all serious evaluation, this is a constant and dynamic process and suggests that there is never a moment when a person knows they have achieved mastery or developed control over any particular process. Rather every experience is a new developmental moment. Learning, teaching, and reading are always in the state of becoming.

10 Real/natural literacy events enhance literacy learning.

For much too long instructional materials have been more concerned with getting ready to read rather than focusing on reading to learn and enjoying both reading and learning. With the growth of an outstanding and ever-growing market of literature written and illustrated for children and adolescents by professional authors and artists, there is no need for artificially created texts for learning to read. In addition, literacy opportunities extend far beyond the world of books. The more readers are involved in reading a wide range of print participating in real life literacy events, the more they will become aware of the power, the necessity, and the joy of literacy.

CONTENT AREA READING

Joan Nelson-Herber and Harold L. Herber

SYRACUSE UNIVERSITY

We have put together the following ten ideas based on our knowledge of the research, our experience working with teachers, and our interest in reading and writing instruction in content areas.

1 Facilitate students' learning with a framework for instruction.

Organization and structure make teaching manageable. Use a framework for instruction that is loose enough to allow for teacher choice and creativity, yet supportive enough to provide a framework and continuity for a variety of research based teaching strategies. For example: we recommend a structure that includes preparation for reading and writing, guidance of the reading and writing processes, and development of independence in reading and writing, as follows:

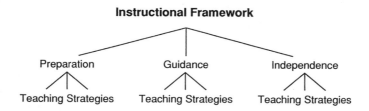

2 Activate students' knowledge of content.

The critical role of prior knowledge in reading comprehension has been amply demonstrated in recent research. What the reader already knows about the content of the text determines to a large extent what is comprehended from the text. In preparing students for reading, use strategies that activate and organize students' knowledge related to or analogous to the subject of study. This can provide a conceptual framework for integrating new ideas from the text with prior knowledge. For example: activate students' prior knowledge by asking them to write down all the words they know related to the topic of study. Help students to organize those words into a semantic map and thus facilitate students' integration of new ideas from the text with their own knowledge and experience.

3   Develop students' knowledge of text structure.

What students know about the structure and organization of a text can also influence what they comprehend from the text. In preparing students for reading, use strategies that make students aware of how the text is structured and how ideas in the text relate to one another. For example: Provide students with a structured overview (graphic organizer, tree diagram, or the like) that uses the vocabulary of the content and shows in skeleton form how the material in the text is organized and how the ideas of the content are related. Use the structured overview to guide students' reading by altering its design, showing only the main elements of the structure and leaving blanks for details of the content to be added during reading. The structured overview under 1 is an example of this kind of strategy.

4   Expand students' vocabulary.

The heavy load of technical vocabulary in content area materials often impedes the students' ability to comprehend the facts and concepts of the subject of study. Use teaching strategies that provide students with knowledge and experience with the technical or uncommon vocabulary of the text before they are expected to recognize that vocabulary in their reading. For example: Identify clusters of words that relate to the concept(s) to be studied. Present and teach these words while constructing the structured overview. Refine students' understandings of the meanings of words from the clusters by including the words in materials such as analogies and various forms of categorization and classification that require students to consider interrelationships that exist among the words.

5   Make students active readers.

Reading is an active, constructive process. Help students to be active readers by using feed-forward teaching strategies. Encourage students to anticipate and predict ideas in the text on the basis of their prior experience and to use their hunches and predictions to guide their own reading. For example: give students a list of statements about the topic and ask them to predict, on the basis of their own knowledge, whether the author of the text would agree with each one. After they have made their predictions, have them read the text to confirm their predictions or refine their knowledge.

6 Develop students' prereading comprehension.

Students often lack background knowledge and experience specific to concepts about to be studied in a content area. Use strategies that create prereading comprehension by building new concepts or by examining conflicting values before requiring students to comprehend them in reading. For example: provide reasoning guides comprised of statements that reflect actions, conditions, or beliefs that have a general bearing on the concepts to be studied. Have students write about and discuss their reasons for accepting or rejecting these statements.

7 Increase students' sophistication in comprehension.

Students do fairly well on literal comprehension, but have difficulty with critical and creative comprehension. Use teaching strategies and instructional materials that extend students' comprehension beyond the literal level. For example: use guide materials that support students' reading and writing at literal, interpretive, and applied levels of comprehension.

8 Help students integrate reading and writing.

Reading and writing are interactive processes. Learning in one mode supports learning in the other mode. Take advantage of this interaction by using both reading and writing to support content learning. For example: have students brainstorm on a concept to be studied and then write a group composition to organize the product of their brainstorming. The result will reflect what they already know about the subject. The writing will help them prepare for reading new text on the subject. Reading the new text will help them improve their writing.

9 Facilitate students' interactive learning.

Cooperative learning increases motivation, facilitates communication, improves academic achievement, enhances self-esteem, and improves interpersonal and intergroup relations. Take advantage of the positive effects of interactive learning by providing students with opportunities to pool their experiences, to discuss ideas, to clarify concepts, as well as opportunities to experience multiple recitation of vocabulary, group composition, and peer tutoring. For example: the activities identified in items 2 and 4-8 above involve students learning interactively in small groups.

10 *Facilitate students' independence.*

Students are always *becoming* independent learners. Teachers help students develop independence in the application of ideas through the processes of refining, extending, and sharing the concepts they have acquired. These processes are logical extensions of instructional strategies used to develop students' proficiency in reading and writing. For example: have students create graphic organizers from word clusters to refine their understanding of concepts previously studied. Have students extend their understanding of a concept by applying a previously discussed reasoning guide to new resources related to the concept. Have students share their understanding of concepts through discussions and writings or share their understanding of learning processes by helping other students refine and extend their own reading and writing proficiencies.

Reading Department
HOFSTRA UNIVERSITY

The following compilation represents a collaborative effort on the part of Harvey Alpert, Sidney J. Rauch, H. Alan Robinson, Lenore Sandel, Janice Studholme, Harold Tanyzer, and Elizabeth Unruh.

1 *Stimulate students to think about their relevant background knowledge when they read or are asked to read about a topic new to them, complex material, or poorly organized material.*

Have them brainstorm out loud or on paper and then do some type of semantic organizing or mapping.

2 *Train students to work with one another in collaborative groups and teams both in reading and in writing.*

Learners should be guided in the revision process, both on what they've composed and what they've comprehended.

3 *Help students develop metacognitive strategies, that is, encourage them to recall and use strategies learned in one or more situations as they turn to novel situations.*

Help students ascertain what they know and what they don't know, as means for finding out what they need to know.

4 *Use a variety of assessment devices of both process and product to learn about the strategies possessed and not possessed by individual students.*

For example, the categories provided by the Miscue Analysis Inventory become exceptionally useful in evaluating cloze insertions, particularly if students have an opportunity to discuss them and to learn to self-evaluate.

5 *Use the language experience approach to capitalize on the language ability and background experiences of the learner.*

This approach enables the teacher to take into consideration the cultural, cognitive, linguistic, and affective factors influencing the reading process, and thereby creates greater proximity between reader and text.

6 *Place increased emphasis on literature as a major element of the reading program.*

Such an approach not only fosters a love of reading but enables teachers to provide opportunities for prediction and similar reading strategies within the context of whole text.

7 *Intervene early in order to reduce the percentage of reading and learning problems.*

Such intervention ought to include the teaching of skills or strategies directly when it becomes evident that individuals or small groups need assistance, and ought to be provided through the material being read or written rather than through isolated pages from workbooks or worksheets.

8 *Use writing to foster deeper interactions with text.*

The use of journals of a variety of types (dialectic, dialogue, team, and personal) not only enhance comprehension but may be used to improve a student's ability to write well and feel good about himself/herself as a writer.

9 *Use a thematic approach to integrate each of the language arts with all of the content areas.*

This approach not only allows for learners to engage in speaking, listening, reading, and writing about a topic, but allows for them to participate in areas where they succeed in order to improve performance in less proficient areas.

10 *Analyze the text structure of the materials used in classrooms.*

Awareness of the difficulties a text may cause will enable teachers to teach readers to process such text. These same readers should also be taught to do a type of text analysis, thereby allowing them to become more independent readers.

Robert Karlin

QUEENS COLLEGE, CUNY

1   *The results of research in reading, although often inconclusive and contradictory, merit study.*

Some research is less flawed than others, and the former might suggest practices that could be tested in the classroom. Moreover, familiarity with the research will reveal the extent to which more and better studies are required before we make definitive judgments about reading and writing instruction.

2   *There is no best, single program for teaching reading.*

Combine features of language experience, individualized, and basal reading to promote reading development.

3   *As a general principle, use what learners know to teach them what they don't know.*

For example, use words students readily recognize to teach them to use phonic and structural analysis for word identification.

4   *To help students master content through reading, integrate the development of comprehension and study skills with their reading of informational materials.*

5   *Use writing activities, such as summarizing and comparing and contrasting, to reinforce what pupils learn through reading.*

6   *Stress flexibility rather than speed of reading.*

Purposes for reading and the nature of materials help to determine how one should read.

7   *Assess computer programs to determine whether they offer instruction or merely practice and the extent to which their content represents current knowledge about the teaching of reading.*

8   *Provide opportunities for oral reading such as sharing books, reading plays and poetry, supporting judgments, and giving instructions.*

9 *Shotgun instruction to overcome reading weaknesses is unproductive.*

Address specific problems with materials that do not present additional difficulties for learners.

10 *Read to students of all ages.*

Encourage and facilitate reading for enjoyment.

Pat Koppman

PDK Associates

1 *Begin each day, or class period, by reading aloud to your students.*

This should be done in classes at all levels (PreK-12). The selections chosen for these sessions should be short ones that can be completed. Instead of worksheets, students can then be assigned activities based on the selection read aloud.

2 *Do not show the illustrations in every book that you read.*

Often the skill of listening can be reinforced better if the pictures are not shared, thus causing the student to create his/her own visual image.

3 *Choose a large blank wall in your classroom to use as a bulletin board.*

Divide the large space into sections slightly larger than 8 1/2 by 11 inches, using thick yarn or strips of construction paper. Label each section with the names of students in your class. (The number of sections you need is determined by the number of students in your class.) Label your bulletin board OUR BEST WORK. Each day before students leave, have them determine which work completed during the day is the best and display it in his/her square on the bulletin board. This allows students to

a. have work displayed each day,

b. assess their own work and make a judgment as to what they want displayed, and

c. feel they have some control over what work is considered to be their best.

4 *Send home a newsletter each Monday.*

The one-page newsletter can be a gameboard, a family field trip suggestion, a recipe, or a suggested book to be shared with the family.

5 *Make homework fun!*

Choose activities that the family can become involved in together but that still allow the student to reinforce skills learned in school.

6 *Send a calendar home each month.*

Use a blank calendar grid. Let students, on the first of each month, write in the name of the month and put dates in the proper places on the calendar. At the bottom or top of the calendar place this question: What have you done with your child today? Suggest that parents and children use the calendar to record activities the family does together (examples: dinner at a fast-food restaurant, a picnic in the park, a walk through the mall, buying and sending a card to a relative or friend).

7 *At a swap meet, garage sale, or used furniture store, purchase a rocking chair.*

Paint the rocker a bright color (mine was yellow!). Sit in the rocker when you read aloud. Prepare a sign-up sheet. Allow students to sign up to use the rocker for their independent reading. The rocker helps reading become a very exciting activity.

8 *Fold or cut plain white butcher paper slightly smaller than the width of a coat hanger.*

The paper can be as long as you wish. On each hanger, list vocabulary words that will be useful to students in their writing. These can be seasonal words, happy words, words to use instead of "said," or scary words. These word charts are easy to store, inexpensive, and quick to make.

9 *Each week introduce a new song to your class.*

One day study the words; the next day, the phrases; and then the individual sentences. Practice sequencing by placing each line of the song in a pocket chart in the appropriate order. At the end of the week, give students each a copy of the song and encourage them to draw an illustration. Let students add each week's song to an ongoing, growing songbook, which can have as many as 30 predictable language and/or rhyming songs.

10 *During language experience time, place a sheet of carbon paper and extra paper behind the sheet you will be using for recording the dictated story of the student.*

After the dictation is completed, remove the carbon and carbon copy. Let the student then trace over the letters, words, and sentences using the carbon copy. There are now two copies of the child's story. One can be used to illustrate, or add to an ongoing book of the child's stories. The other copy can be cut apart and used in many ways: to make word cards for games and/or practice, to rebuild the original story, to rearrange into a different story, to take home for practicing with the family, or to add to a word box that can be used during writing activities.

Eleanor Ladd Kress

Temple University, Retired

Essentials of a training program for elementary teachers—individuals who have a mature understanding of themselves and who like children! They compose a program for anyone wishing to become a reading teacher at any level.

Develop

1 a workable knowledge of child developmental theory and principles.

2 an understanding of the psychology of learning (Piaget and Bruner) and of individual differences.

3 an in-depth knowledge of children's literature.

4 a sound awareness of the history of the teaching of reading.

5 a comparative survey of teaching methods.

6 the ability to use and interpret Informal Reading Inventories and other informal tests that yield information designed to assist with instruction.

Examine

7 a wide variety of available materials (narrative, expository and reference) and develop a set of criteria for evaluating them.

Demonstrate

8 competence in teaching a language experience (and/or whole language) approach, including:

a. using familiar songs, stories poems

b. taking dictation (individual and group)

c. organizing word banks for students to use for a variety of purposes

d. making books of children's writings

e. keeping progress charts

9   competence in planning and executing lessons for teaching a single skill, such as comprehension or word recognition, utilizing knowledge of learning sequences:

a. known to unknown

b. concrete to abstract

c. gross to fine

d. simple to complex

e. auditory to visual

f. similarities to differences

This is the HOW of teaching—the HOW of simplifying. Two successfully completed eight-step lessons written by teachers (one for a word recognition skill and one for a comprehension skill) enable them to understand sequencing:

a. Auditory - concrete - similarities

b. Auditory - concrete - differences

c. Auditory - abstract - similarities

d. Auditory - abstract - differences

e. Auditory-visual - concrete - similarities

f. Auditory-visual - concrete - differences

g. Auditory-visual - abstract - similarities

h. Auditory-visual - abstract - differences

These lessons reveal a powerful teaching method when written inductively (no telling) and demand much change from previous concepts of "teaching." Videotaping of these lessons when possible and subsequent discussion promote growth. Each concrete lesson focuses on real objects or examples. Note that only one characteristic of the lesson is changed at a time as the sequence progresses in complexity. Children often demonstrate that they are able to perform competently at the auditory levels and do not start to become insecure until the written word is added at the auditory-visual step (e). Lessons should have an introduction in which the task to be learned is discovered by the students, time to practice is provided, and at the end of the lesson convergence on the specific task to be learned is brought about through statements of the students. Three often-asked focusing questions are:

What have you learned?

How do you know?

What will you expect next time?

10 competence in teaching a directed reading-thinking activity (within the single lesson the student progresses from instructional level to independent level for the material used).

  a. Preparation

- select material (basal, content areas, trade books, reference material, current events, magazines, classroom writings)
- establish teacher purposes
- collect suppplementary materials to foster interest
- identify new vocabulary and concepts
- formulate possible higher-order questions

  b. Readiness

- assist in re-examination of previous background to approximate sufficient readiness (through discussion, mapping, webbing, clustering, brainstorming, concept development, and/or vocabulary development)
- help each student set an individual purpose

  c. Silent Reading

- observe and assist student to recognize when purpose is accomplished
- make diagnostic observations

  d. Discussion

- clarify adequacy of information gained
- assist students in formulating their own questions as related to purposes established
- ask higher-order questions to enhance thinking skills
- demonstrate to students that they made judgments and inferences

  e. Follow-up

- provide opportunities to extend and broaden skills and concepts identified in lesson

Susan Lytle and Morton Botel

University of Pennsylvania

We have four fundamental assumptions about language, literacy, and learning on which experiential framework is based, which are presented as the first four best ideas.

1   The first assumption is the centrality of learning to *meaning-making*, the notion that effective readers, writers, and speakers use language actively and constructively to gain new ideas and insights.

2   The second assumption is the concept that language is inherently *social*, that language use occurs in a situation, and that learning takes place in the context of a community of learners. Instruction at all levels and in all content areas needs to reflect attention to creating communities of readers, writers, and talkers.

3   The third assumption emphasizes the *interrelationships of the language processes*—of reading, writing, listening, and speaking. Oral and written language should be continuously related; learners become skillful by using language for authentic, communicative purposes.

4   The fourth assumption focuses on learning as *human* activity. Readers and writers bring to the language processes their own prior knowledge and belief systems, which they orchestrate in ways unique to themselves.

Building on these four assumptions, the next five ideas are presented as critical experiences.

5   *Reading is transacting with text.*

Reading includes encountering texts that embody different purposes, concepts, and structures; using a repertoire of strategies for a variety of purposes; bringing critical and creative questions to the text and being willing to take risks; and responding in a variety of ways: discussions, enactments, writing, and the use of other media.

6   *Writing is composing texts.*

Writing includes acquiring a repertoire of composing processes; selecting the strategies most appropriate for different kinds of discourse, audiences, and purposes for writing; and using writing to learn content, to engage actively in the study of a discipline, and to make sense of and affect the world.

7 *Reading and writing should be extended beyond the content in which they occur in school.*

Students should: choose among options what to read and write in and out of school, as a part of the regular program; use reading and writing to satisfy personal and social needs; and develop a variety of strategies depending on the text, context, and their own purposes.

8 *Language should be explored in the context of language in use, not as a discrete set of skills.*

Metalinguistic awareness should be acquired, including knowledge about language and how it functions, knowledge of the structures of language (systems or parts and how they are related to each other), and knowledge of the social rules of language use. Students should do problem-solving tasks with whole texts, deal with the parts only within a meaningful context, and seek information about language forms and functions in order to accomplish communicative purposes. In addition students should understand relationships between language and culture, appreciate cultural and linguistic diversity in the classroom, and learn about different styles of language appropriate for different circumstances.

9 *Students should be taught to learn how to learn.*

This facility includes metacognition and meta-comprehension strategies, learning to function independently and interdependently, learning to pose as well as solve problems, and generating appropriate questions and responding appropriately to questions.

10 *Integrative models of curriculum and learning are more likely to be successful if the evaluation program reflects these models.*

"Designing Congruent Evaluation" incorporates the following ideas: Evaluation should interrelate language skills and content. It should put major emphasis on observation to assess student learning. It should focus on dimensions of student behavior that relate to improving performance. It should provide information for teachers, parents, and students about the students' evolving personal structures of knowledge. It should involve students in assessing their own work and the efforts of their peers. Evaluation strategies should be differentiated in order to address the needs and purposes of various constituencies.

Eve Malmquist

UNIVERSITY OF LINKOPING, SWEDEN

The development of reading ability should no longer be looked upon as an isolated technical problem of instruction. It should rather be considered a complex process ongoing during an individual's whole lifetime from early infancy to old adult age. There is a dynamic interaction between an individual's physical, intellectual, emotional, and social development and the development of reading ability. Reading skills of different kinds have become increasingly vital factors in adjusting to life in every corner of our world today. Success or failure in attaining elementary reading proficiency may affect the individual's entire behavior and attitude towards his or her environment. A failure in the early stages of learning to read seems to be closely related to emotional disturbances and personality difficulties of various kinds. It is extremely difficult, however, to determine whether personality difficulties are the causes, effects, or only concomitant factors of reading disabilities.

1 *Reading ability is a series of complex mental activities.*

Reading ability is not a unitary skill, but rather a series of complex mental activities, which vary with the reader's age and maturity, the kind and degree of difficulty of the reading material, and the purpose of reading. In a psychological sense, the reading process includes all that happens from the moment we start to react to the visual stimuli—the written or printed words—up to our responses to these stimuli in the form of thoughts, feelings, spoken or written words, or actions of various kinds.

2 *Language development in the early years influences reading comprehension.*

The development of the ability of understanding and getting meaning out of language is a lifetime process, extending from infancy through adulthood.

There is enough evidence to give us reason to state that a child's progress in learning to read is largely dependent upon his experiences with the use of the spoken word in his preschool years.

Thinking and language develop in intimate interaction.

For most children, learning to read is the very first encounter with a type of learning involving abstract symbols, which are intended to be associated with previous experiences. If the child has not been given the opportunities to acquire such a background of meaningful concepts, and if the words presented in print are not a part of his speaking vocabulary or are used with inadequate understanding, his or her reading efforts will be handicapped from the very beginning.

3 Early diagnosis and treatment are the keynotes in teaching reading comprehension.

Because of the great differences in maturation and abilities among children of the same age, a fixed chronological age should not be used as the criterion of a child's readiness for school entry and learning to read. It seems to me that a flexible time for starting school and a slow and successive introduction of pupils from the preschool to the school is the only reasonable administrative policy to follow, in order to diminish the number of cases of reading failures.

Every child should be given the opportunity to feel the great satisfaction and motivation for continued work that is connected with success. That means that the teacher must make sure, both in the beginning and all the way through school, that the child's capacities match the task she or he is expected to perform.

The need for organizing instruction to provide for children's individual differences is evident and urgent. To provide learning steps, methods, and procedures suited to the individual learner, the teacher has to use a diagnostic approach.

4 Prevent reading disabilities by using reading readiness programs.

Many children who fail at school in the introductory learning activities are human songbirds who never learned how to sing, as an old proverb in my country expresses it. Language is a tool of learning.

It should be in the greatest interest of every nation to increase efforts toward the *prevention* of reading disabilities, thereby diminishing the need of economically expensive remediation later on. An important step should be a fully articulated reading and writing readiness program that begins by age three or four and includes the combined efforts of parents, preschool, and school. An elementary reading and writing program in most languages should be based upon the following prerequisites:

a. the child can *listen* attentively to sounds and linguistic signals;

b. the child can imitate and *understand* these signals;

c. the child can *speak* reasonably well;

d. the child's *vocabulary* is sufficiently large;

e. the child can distinguish and discriminate *visually*; and

f. the child's *motor capacity* is sufficiently developed.

5 Reading development can be predicted.

Many investigators have stressed the significance of early diagnosis, which might make early treatment of potential cases of reading disability possible. But there is a lack of acceptable prediction instruments in most countries. Also, very few acceptably controlled longitudinal studies have been made of the effects of early identification and treatment of reading disabilities. It would be helpful to have more longitudinal research studies of this type in various countries and language spheres around the world.

6 Reading comprehension should be viewed in a broad perspective.

Reading comprehension does not denote a single, well-defined aspect of reading ability. It is dependent on: the reader's personal competencies in different aspects, including a number of basic reading skills; the reader's degree of attention to and interest in the content; the reader's knowledge and experiences concerning the presented material; the reader's needs and expectations of what the reading might offer; and the reader's emotional engagement, interpretation, and critical thinking.

We should put reading comprehension in a broad perspective in many different ways. Adequate instruction for the improvement of abilities in listening, speaking, or writing will be of great value also for the development of reading skills, such as those that involve thinking, decision-making, problem-solving, critical evaluation, and creativity.

7 Comprehension skills should be taught throughout all school levels.

The concept of reading readiness should be applied not only to the beginning stages of reading but to all levels in all subjects and throughout adult life. The teacher is expected to ask, at all points, whether the individual is adequately mature to grasp the content of the reading text, whether he or she can integrate it with earlier knowledge and experiences, and whether he or she can understand the reading and put that understanding to use. This continuous diagnostic approach should also be applied to the teacher's guidance of the student's development and to the student's interests and tastes in recreational reading in or out of school.

8 Special vocabulary and special kinds of thinking in each subject area should be taught.

We should not take for granted that students who otherwise master the basic mechanics of reading shall also be able to make effective use of all the different kinds of supportive devices that are included in the text to help them understand, learn, and observe better. In most instances it is necessary to give them systematically arranged exercises as well as adequate instruction on how to profit from such resources.

Every subject has its special vocabulary that the student has to acquire. It often takes a very long time before a child reaches the point at which she or he can begin to make generalizations and comprehend abstract concepts. This developmental process progresses only gradually. Students should be stimulated to seek the support and further knowledge that they require in order to understand a special term.

The reaction and approach to reading texts must vary in accordance with the nature and the purpose of the reading. It is therefore essential that the special reading technique that is required in a certain subject be carefully explained and exercised in a continuous and systematic fashion under the guidance of a competent teacher.

9 Observation and criticism of various kinds of propaganda should be taught.

Students should be taught to observe and critically evaluate different kinds of propaganda. Advertisements in newspapers and magazines make excellent and stimulating reading materials for such exercises.

We must teach our students to be watchful and not to draw inaccurate conclusion on the bases of data that are no longer acceptable. Reading in a true sense of the word calls for *active thinking*. We must therefore make our students base their reading in independent thinking; they must learn to deliberate, examine, and judge as they read.

10 *A third dimension in the reading comprehension process is creative thinking.*

Sometimes critical reading and creative reading are brought into the same category. Creative reading often includes imagination, fantasy and free associations. Critical reading always requires some kind of evaluation and judgment. It might be appropriate to divide the reading comprehension skills into three main categories: receptive reading, critical reading, and creative reading. We use receptive reading to locate and identify facts, opinions, and reports that the author has presented. A student who is to be able to read creatively or critically must possess the receptive reading skills. By creative reading I mean the capacity to reach beyond what the writer has been able to transfer onto the printed page, and to go beyond criticizing and evaluating. I am referring to the capacity to look forward, to search, and to asking pertinent and vital questions to come up with *new discoveries* in thought and feeling. Teachers must foster the ability of their pupils to put forward *new questions and new problems*. Creative reading is often divided in two categories: divergent creative reading and convergent creative reading. In divergent creative reading we use the ideas of the author as a springboard for new ideas. In convergent creative reading we use the knowledge and experiences of the author in addition to our own in order to process an existing solution of a problem.

Anthony V. Manzo

UNIVERSITY OF MISSOURI, KANSAS CITY

Ideas are personal. They tend to have little life outside a given set of assumptions. The ideas expressed here are the ones that have guided my own teaching, research, and professional perspectives. To that extent, this listing might better be called "Ten Ideas That Have Been Useful to Me."

It might be helpful, in considering them for yourself, to note one thing that they all tend to have in common: the belief that teaching must be satisfying for the teacher as well as for the student. This is no mean accomplishment when it is realized that learning means changing. And changing involves a certain amount of resistance: minds are urged, on a daily basis, to do just a little more than they are able to do with comfort. The teacher must prod and praise, all in some delicate balance that must also be self-satisfying, to keep teaching stimulating and healthy.

1 Modeling

Modeling in education means providing a tangible demonstration of a behavior that otherwise would be internal and unobservable. Effective modeling has the additional benefit of creating a sense of felt need. The particular behavior demonstrated can be seen as both reachable and desirable. Used regularly, modeling is a means of bringing apprenticeship training, so common in other areas of learning, into the classroom.

2 Reciprocity

Reciprocity is a characteristic of a classroom interaction which emerges when students are encouraged to "poke back" and subtly influence the direction of a lesson in an interactive and nonbelligerent manner. When coupled with modeling, reciprocity tends to raise the student's sense of felt need and to promote active learning and responding.

3 ReQuest Procedure

The ReQuest, or Reciprocal Questioning Procedure (Manzo, 1969) and Reciprocal Teaching (Palincsar and Brown, 1986), are reading comprehension teaching methods that seamlessly bring together modeling and reciprocity in a form that is relatively easy to use in almost any classroom situation. These methods are most notable for their robust nature and the emphasis they place on teaching students to be strategic readers.

4 Gray's Paradigm for Teaching Phonic Elements

Everything one ever needs to know about the principles of teaching phonics is clearly represented in Gray's Paradigm for Teaching Phonic Elements. It offers a universally applicable, five-step procedure for teaching any phonic element (Gray, 1948; Manzo and Manzo, 1990).

5 Glass Analysis

The Glass Analysis procedure offers the simplest way I know to teach decoding without teaching phonics rules. It can be used with minimal training by anyone who knows how to read (Glass and Glass, 1973; Manzo and Manzo, 1990).

6 Directed Reading-Thinking Activity (DR-TA)

Stauffer's DR-TA is a basic paradigm to guide pre-, during-, and post-reading comprehension, thinking, and skill development. It is a master plan for most other contemporary methods of guiding reading comprehension (Stauffer, 1969; Shepherd, 1982; Manzo and Manzo, 1990).

7 Read, Encode, Annotate, Ponder (REAP)

The REAP procedure was one of the first strategies to offer a means for easily connecting reading, writing, and thinking. It also offers some useful formats for teaching students how to think critically and respond to text (Eanet and Manzo, 1976; Manzo and Manzo, 1990).

8 Motor Imaging

Motor Imaging is a vocabulary teaching method that offers an innovative means of learning vocabulary by stimulating sensorimotor associations as well as cognitive and affective engagement with words. (Casale, 1985; Manzo and Manzo, 1990).

9 Concurrent Methods

Concurrent methods create instructional efficiency by simultaneously promoting more than one educational objective at a time. More specifically, they are designed to nourish elements of general human development, such as the ability to critique and be critiqued, objectivity, and personal-social adjustment, along with academic objectives. These elements often appear slight when compared with the teaching of reading, writing, and arithmetic, but their impact on all aspects of academic and emotional maturity can be compared to the value of trace elements like zinc, potassium, and iron to human physical nutrition and growth (Manzo and Manzo, 1990).

10 Heuristics

Heuristic methods lead teachers as well as students to self-explore the best means by which to teach and learn. Methods such as the Lecture-Read-Discuss heuristic are hands-on, learn-by-doing approaches that cause teachers to learn about teaching while teaching. They are easily adopted and adapted (Manzo and Casale, 1985; Manzo and Manzo, 1990).

Robert A. McCracken

McCRACKEN EDUCATIONAL SERVICES, SURREY, BRITISH COLUMBIA

1   In 1948 I first became acquainted with the "fact" that knowledge of letters and letter sounds was an important prerequisite in learning to read. In the next few years I learned the importance of word recognition in learning to read and was introduced to the age-old and continuing argument about phonics versus look-say methodologies.

2   In 1953 I met a six-year-old boy who read avidly with excellent comprehension. He did not know that the alphabet existed. He knew the names of only three letters: A, I, and X. I asked him how he learned to read and he said, "My father read A. A. Milne's poems to me, and after I learned them I just took the books and figured out how the words worked." I asked him how he learned an unknown word and he said, "I just ask someone who knows." "What if you forget?" I asked. He replied, "I don't forget." (One small puncture in the dike of traditional truth.)

3   In 1956 I asked a five-year-old boy if he could read. He said, "I can read lots of books, but I don't know any words yet. Would you like to hear my favorite book?" He brought two books which he read orally with great enthusiasm and perfect word recognition. (Another puncture.)

4   Sometime in the early 1970s I became conscious that I often saw or heard what I expected to see or hear rather than what was there. In May of 1989 I read: "By now the nebular hypothesis was so successful that a bandwagon syndrome took over and astronomers began seeing what they thought they ought to see." (Ferris, Timothy. *Coming of Age in the Milky Way*, p. 166. Wm. Morrow, New York: 1988.)

5   In 1974 a seven-year-old boy in grade two told me, "Reading is getting the thoughts of others about things."

6   I can't date when I first heard or read Frank Smith say that you learn to read by reading.

7   This leads us to a realization that we are all products of our experiences, and that when we believe what we are taught we act upon those beliefs in two ways:

a. We try to behave so that we act in accordance with our beliefs.

b. We see almost all events in ways that our beliefs are not disturbed. When something peculiar happens we ignore it as much as possible, and if we cannot ignore it we interpret the peculiarity so that it is consistent with what we think it should be.

8   I am led to the possibility that recognizing words is the result of having learned to read, and concentrating only on learning words, or predominantly on learning words, interferes with the whole process of reading and learning to read. I just listen to music. I didn't learn how to listen to the notes first. I listen to the meanings in conversation, not to the words. In learning to speak children listen to meanings; attention to individual words comes after speech has begun, perhaps much after. I just watch films or television, not the frames or the dots that make up the images. As a reader I pay attention to meanings, not to the words, unless the meaning is distorted out of expectation. How else can I read orally without error at first sight, "The does have no antlers but the buck does" or "He wound the bandage around the wound"?

9   What if we could instill in our students, particularly those destined to become teachers, the understanding that even though we professors know the research and are unbiased in our assessments of truth, we believe in our theories and methods as Einstein did when asked how he would have felt if the results of an astronomical observation did not confirm his theory: "I would have had to pity our dear Lord. The theory is correct." (Rosenthal-Schneider, Ilse. *Reality and Scientific Truth*, p. 74. Detroit: Wayne State University, 1980.)

10   Perhaps Sylvia Ashton-Warner was more correct than even she believed when she said that if the child has enough meaning in the brain (she said within the organic being), one look at a word fixed it for life.

11   (I know that there were to be only ten items, but I need eleven.) Perhaps the brain's accretion of the melodies and meanings of literature empower the eye to seek meaning on the page, enabling the child to read with little attention to the words, letters, or letter-sounds; thus through a process of apprehension and trial and error a child may come to recognize words as a result of learning how to read.

Lee Mountain

UNIVERSITY OF HOUSTON

Ten best ideas? The more I thought upon it,
The more I saw them capsuled in sonnet.

1 Make pleasure reading your primary mission,

2 But still teach phonics and sight recognition.

3 When reading to your students, be dramatic.

4 Stock up on books; raid basement, shelf, and attic.

5 Encourage kids to join book clubs and spend;

6 Be sure they choose books they can comprehend.

7 Don't sneer at basals or at teacher's guides;

8 Use all the help each lesson plan provides.

9 Find methods that make study seem like play.

10 Make time for free-choice reading every day.

With these ideas, your students will be blest;
They'll have the reading teacher who's the best.

Wayne Otto

University of Wisconsin, Madison

You can call me a case of arrested development, but ask me to list ten of almost anything and I'm likely to start talking in terms of Thou Shalts and Thou Shalt Nots. It's the old Sunday School influence and it persists in spite of a perfectly plausible story I once heard—or maybe it's *because* of the story that I'm hung up on the Shalts and Shalt Nots.

Even as Moses took the last few steps down the mountain and began to speak to his people about the tablets he was carrying, so the story goes, he slipped on a loose rock and dropped one of the tablets, which shattered into even more pieces than there are sparrows to keep an eye on. So as Moses spake, this is how it went: Behold, my brethren; I bring you fifteen—oops—ten commandments.

Now I'm not saying I *believe* there was another tablet; but that hasn't kept me from wondering what might have been on it. What if it had said something like "Don't worry; be happy"? Or, maybe, "Grab your coat and get your hat; leave your worries on the doorstep. Just direct your feet to the sunny side of the street." Things might have turned out a lot better for us.

Or, then again, maybe not.

I tell you all this for two reasons. First, in spite of a deep-seated personal inclination, I haven't found *do's* and *don't's* very useful in contemplating my list of ten ideas. And second, even though I'm not sure what would be on my list if it were a little longer, I can't help thinking that if it were it might have turned out a lot better.

Or then again, maybe not.

What turns out to be on my LIST OF TEN, instead of straightforward Shalts and Shalt Nots, is an aggregation of conundrums to contemplate, dilemmas to get off the horns of, admonitions to heed, and a couple of suggestions. Admonitions and suggestions could be taken as *do's* and *don't's*, I suppose; but I really don't intend them to be so stark. The longer I remain in the reading game, the less disposed I am to engage in very much pontificating. I'm inclined to think in terms of "things you ought to keep in mind if you're going to try to teach real people to read real-world materials." So here are my ten ideas for reading teachers: three admonitions, three dilemmas, two conundrums and two suggestions.

1 *If you're going to teach reading for very long, you ought to think about the type of literacy you're trying to develop.*

It seems fashionable these days to point out that there are many "literacies." I do believe that people who take on the task of teaching reading need to give serious thought to whether it's *functional, cultural* or *critical* literacy they intend to pursue. Traditionally, reading teachers have been content, by default if not by design, to settle for functional literacy, or what some people call basic school-based literacy. I think that reading teachers could offer much more to literacy development and that individual teachers ought to think carefully about what "more" could mean to them.

2 *If you're going to teach reading in the public schools, beware of three apocalyptic horsemen: basal readers, grade level, and standardized achievement tests.*

Together, these three amount to a force almost as irresistible as the fabled Four Horsemen of the Apocalypse. They prescribe what reading instruction is, when it should be offered, and what constitutes success. They reduce teachers to slavish page-turners and students to a least common denominator. Listen to the siren song of the Three Horsemen and you'll be lured to the Land of the Living Dead.

3 *If you believe that children—adults, too—have a life outside of school, try not to confuse healthy adaptations with pathologies.*

With the Three Horsemen firmly seated, many deviations from the "norm" of school-learning behavior are likely to be seen as "problems" that range from personal to social to physical. Oftentimes such "deviant" behaviors are in fact remarkably sensible adaptations to conflicts between school reality and personal reality. Such adaptations should be seen as positive, not negative signs.

4 *Come to grips with the dilemma of collective instruction.*

Classroom teachers who aim to get each child to read to the best of his or her ability must do two things: First, provide instruction for everyone and second, address individual differences among students. The problem is to treat students similarly (to provide reading instruction to everyone) and at the same time to treat them differently (to address each one's differences). The solution, if there is one, must involve striking a working balance between sameness—efficient instruction for the group—and diversity—differentiated instruction for individuals.

5 Come to grips with the dilemma of professional uncertainty.

The horns of this dilemma are, on one side, the expectation that everyone will learn (be taught) to read at some prescribed level, and on the other side, the fact that nobody is sure how children learn how to read or how best to teach them. A positive step in the right direction is to recognize that one's personal knowledge and beliefs about teaching must forever remain subject to revision and change.

6 Come to grips with the specific vs. strategic knowledge dilemma.

Here the horns of the dilemma are, on one side, specific knowledge (what Hirsch calls *basic knowledge of the culture* and others call *declarative or specialized domain knowledge*) and on the other side, strategic knowledge (Hirsch says *skills-oriented* and others say *procedural* or *general strategic*). The dilemma posed for reading teachers is whether the main thrust of reading instruction ought to be carried by wide, carefully guided reading or by the development of transferable, across-the-curriculum skills and strategies. Both the problem and the solution seem to lie in seeking some reasonable balance. Such a solution would be a step in the right direction because, traditionally, reading teachers have been disinclined to get very deeply involved in directing the acquisition of domain-specific knowledge. Hirsch says we've been satisfied to teach skills in content-free, or perhaps more accurately, content-barren contexts.

7 When you do tackle strategy instruction, ask yourself, "strategies for what?"

"Strategy instruction" is a big fashion item this season; everybody's talking about it. But hardly anybody is acknowledging that in addition to being applied in various content areas, strategies must be applied in specific classroom contexts. What's lost in the shuffle is consideration of the criterion task—in other words, *what's to be tested by a given teacher*. There's plenty of evidence to show that certain strategies work when motivated students know the criterion task; but the same strategies don't help much when the criterion task isn't known by the learner. In real classrooms students seldom know the criterion task, and teachers often haven't given much thought to the criterion task either. If you, the reading teacher, are going to succeed in helping students develop effective strategies for reading and learning, you *must* line up your efforts with criterion tasks as they are set and perceived in real classrooms.

8   *After you've decided to teach "phonics," you still must ask yourself, "How?"*

Let's assume, for the sake of argument, that the great debate has been resolved and there's general agreement that in order to read textual material one must decode print matter. And let's recklessly assume, too, that there is general agreement that one teaches decoding by offering phonics (letter-sound associations) instruction. Now, even with these far-from-agreed-upon agreements hypothetically in place it is still a fact that there is very little agreement on how to proceed with instruction. Suggestions range all the way from writing-to-read approaches that encourage and refine invented spellings, to see-and-say approaches that proceed through analysis of sight words in experience stories, to grunt-and-spit approaches that proceed through letter-sound synthesis via countless rules and exceptions.

Certainly I'm not here to suggest the ultimate "how to." I merely suggest that there are other ways to teach phonics than with workbooks, tapes, kits and commercially prepared programs. And I do believe that, given thoughtful choosing, most any "other" is a better choice.

9   *It's at least as important to help developing readers attain fluency in their reading as to help them become efficient decoders.*

In terms of Chall's stages, after beginning readers have gotten glued to print they've got to get unglued in order to continue to make progress. In other words, once beginning readers have realized the role and function of the actual print in the reading process and how to cope with it, they need to set themselves free to concentrate on getting meaning. They must become fast, accurate—*fluent*—readers with the courage and skill to use context as well as print itself.

Samuels has argued long and eloquently that it is this attainment of *automaticity* in word identification that enables readers to redirect attention from getting the words to getting the meaning.

Samuels recommends repeated reading as a specific technique for developing automaticity. Chall and many others point out the need for wide reading of easy, familiar materials to develop fluency. The essential point is that teachers need to give explicit, systematic, and persistent attention to helping novice readers—mainly by setting aside sufficient time and providing guidance in selection of appropriate materials—to attain fluency/automaticity. It's an essential developmental stage that must not be neglected.

10 *Beware of all enterprises that provide outside-the-classroom "help" for your readers.*

Someplace in Walden, Thoreau says, "Beware of all enterprises that require new clothes."

Now it may be a vast leap from Thoreau's line to mine, but I think the upshot is the same. In my observations, novice readers who get sent out to special programs usually wind up in strange places ("enrichment" classes, corrective-remedial classes, or shudder, LD rooms) that they were ill-chosen to be in for purposes that serve special interests (turf building, meeting quotas implicitly imposed by outside funding, getting respite from bad behavior, catering to pressure groups, etc., etc., etc.) much better than the readers'. I'm convinced that, in almost all instances, the most effective reading instruction is likely to be offered in the regular classroom. By teachers in comfortable clothes.

So that's my list. I want it to be more of an invitation to ask *why* than a list that tells *what* or *how*. I hope it is.

P. David Pearson

UNIVERSITY OF ILLINOIS AT URBANA-CHAMPAIGN

1   Whenever you teach something—a skill, a strategy, a routine, or an idea—make sure it helps kids understand the story they are reading today, *but don't feel like you've accomplished much until it gets used voluntarily in the story they read* tomorrow.

2   The best justification for assessing students' performance today is to enable them to assess their own tomorrow.

3   Assess students by observation as well as by standardized tests.

When tests didn't occupy the position of importance that today's high stakes accountability schemes have afforded them, their instructional validity didn't matter too much; after all nobody really taught to them directly. But high stakes accountability has changed all that; people teach to tests regardless of how well they serve the role of a blueprint for a curriculum. So tests now bear a burden never before required of them. They must be worth "teaching to"; they must stand the test of instructional authenticity. Teachers who learn to trust and to document their own judgments will be a step ahead on the path to our next generation of literacy assessments.

4   There is no more important advice for all teachers than the adage, "Learning proceeds from the known to the new."

This adage is at the heart of all comprehension and learning. It explains how children learn, why they fail when they don't, how we should arrange experiences to facilitate new learning, and what makes a good teacher good. It also explains why analogies, metaphors, and examples are so powerful. It is the heart of vocabulary instruction, the soul of comprehension, and the lifeblood of concept development. It is even true for learning phonics skills! You can only learn what is new in terms of what you already know; there is no other choice. The quicker we learn that lesson as teachers, the sooner we'll quit complaining about what kids don't know and get on with the business of taking advantage of what they do know.

5   *Begin and end every reading lesson in the students' world, not your own.*

At the beginning, it means engaging background knowledge to start things off. At the end of a lesson, it means making sure that students get a chance to *use* whatever they've learned so that it belongs to them rather than to you.

Lillian R. Putnam

KEAN COLLEGE, UNION, NEW JERSEY

1   Make a thorough diagnosis of the student's strengths and weaknesses before beginning instruction. Include:

  a. Present reading levels.

  b. Knowledge and use of specific skills in decoding.

  c. Knowledge and use of context clues, sight words, and general vocabulary.

  d. General language ability.

  e. Comprehension abilities.

  f. Ability to organize both narrative and expository material.

2   Determine strengths/weaknesses in modality—that is, auditory, visual, tactile, and kinesthetic processes.

    With severe cases, usually tracing, copying, and writing make the task concrete and vary the pathways within the brain. At the minimum, they secure and hold attention.

3   If the method used thus far has failed, chances are that another method or a different approach should be tried first. For instance, a child who cannot learn words holistically as units may be able to cope with individual letters better.

4   Instructions should be aimed at the student's level, not at a grade or expected level. Nothing succeeds like success.

5   Be certain the student understands *what* you are teaching and why and *how* it will help him.

6   Teach for transfer by (a) providing similar or identical elements in two tasks, and (b) helping the student see the similarities. Skills are learned best when applied in context, or in settings as similar to the natural use as possible.

7   From Grade 4 on, when expository text is stressed, reading instruc-

tion should stress good study skills, such as vocabulary, main ideas, and organization.

8   The oral language that children bring to the reading process has a powerful effect on their success. The expressive and receptive vocabularies evident in listening, speaking, and writing have a profound influence on reading ability. As teachers we must use all these language arts to promote reading.

9   We read for only two reasons, to get information or for pleasure. The sheer joy and pleasure of reading is usually subsumed in the information-getting procedure. We need to demonstrate the enchantment and pleasure of good literature from preschool levels through all the grades, not by talking about good literature, but by exposing students to it.

10   Learning to read is a lifetime process. It improves as we practice.

Annette T. Rabin

LINCOLN UNIVERSITY, PENNSYLVANIA

As a reading specialist at the secondary level, and as a teacher of college reading students and those who will be teaching reading to others, my concern has always been that the "real world" is too often not brought into the reading classroom.

I suggest the following ways of correlating the skills taught in the reading class with those needed to survive in the content area classroom and, in some instances, outside of school.

1   Teach vocabulary that will be useful in the various disciplines. Relevant word elements, especially, can be the focus.

2   When teaching purpose-setting questions, arrange with the social studies teacher to work together on a chapter that has been planned for the course, doing some of the actual work in the reading classroom. Have students turn the chapter title and subheadings into *who, what, when, why,* or *how* questions and then read to answer them.

3   Plan a library research project with the science teacher, doing the research during the time scheduled for reading class so that students can be directed to reference materials on their individual levels.

4   Teach critical reading skills using the newspaper. Ads, editorials, political cartoons, and during election periods, political speeches make excellent subject matter, and at the same time endow students with a little sales resistance and keep them apprised of current events.

5   Teach previewing skills using the actual textbooks that the students are using in their content area classes. This serves the dual purpose of teaching the skill while acquainting the students with the format of their own text and the presence of valuable study aids, such as a glossary or specialized appendices.

6   Send a flyer to the faculty offering to evaluate any textbook that they may be considering for adoption for readability, format, and concept level.

7   Borrow the class list of a teacher who is concerned about the poor progress of a particular class. From the records of their most recent standardized test scores, determine the number of students reading at each grade level. Then compute the readability level of the text-book being used in the class. Offer to help that teacher with some content-area reading strategies.

8   Offer to do an inservice presentation for content-area teachers in your school during which you demonstrate such skills as previewing, advance organizers, and the DR-TA, and explain their benefits.

9   Convince content-area teachers that it is a good idea to start the year by administering a cloze test based on a section from the projected major textbook for the year to help them know which students will need the most reinforcement if they are to succeed with the material.

10 Look at the student as a whole person. If he/she makes little or no progress despite all of your efforts, don't hesitate to seek the assistance of the school nurse, counselor, or psychologist to do any testing or diagnosis for which you have no resources or talents.

Peggy E. Ransom

BALL STATE UNIVERSITY, MUNCIE, INDIANA

1   *The First Grade Studies* (Bond and Dykstra, 1967) are a very good reminder to teachers that they, not the approach, make the difference. Even now people are looking for a panacea, and this helps them understand that they are the important element in teaching.

2   Durkin's studies, *Time on Task*, have given teachers a way to analyze their organizational plans for teaching reading. Along with these studies, her work on the questioning techniques used in basal readers helps teachers realize that they do focus on factual questions too much.

3   The language experience approach is the best basic idea for reading. I realize that *whole language* is the key phrase now, but the theory is the same. The usage of literature and basals is not new and is an excellent idea for teachers.

4   The ideas that comprehension is connected to prior knowledge, and that students can be made aware of their comprehension as they read, are a real help to reading teachers. (Sometimes the latter is called *Reciprocal Teaching* or *Comprehension Monitoring*.)

5   Strategies for teaching reading in the content areas like Hal Herber's studies help teachers understand and teach students how to read and study with expository material.

6   Informal Assessments like the cloze test and the Informal Reading Inventory are useful tools for diagnosing students' reading abilities.

7   Clymer's study on generalizations and other studies that have followed it provide insight for reading teachers.

8   Fry's readability graph has been an accurate tool for both elementary and secondary reading teachers. Its simple form has helped pinpoint the difficulty of some materials. Like any tool, it can be overused, but over time, it has proven its worth in the classroom.

9   Emergent literacy, or combining writing with learning to read, is gaining validity in the reading classroom. Clay's studies on children's writing are now reaching a broader audience and helping them understand reading readiness.

10 Literacy is the birthright of every human being. The idea that literacy is a lifetime development has also awakened many reading teachers. The teaching of reading extends from birth to death, and one school year is just a small part of the process.

Richard Robinson

UNIVERSITY OF MISSOURI, COLUMBIA

Joycelin Hulett

COLUMBIA PUBLIC SCHOOLS

1 The Directed Reading Activity

The directed reading lesson has shown itself to be a practical, useful plan for reading instruction that has met the test of time.

2 Written Conversation

Written conversation brings together other writing and reading procedures such as invented spelling, reading for meaning, and the importance of each individual's background as a foundation for all meaningful language.

3 Sustained Silent Reading

Sustained silent reading is highly motivational because it encourages reading that is meaningful to the individual as opposed to reading as an academic subject.

4 Metacomprehension

Metacomprehension, or the cognitive self-appraisal of what is understood when reading, has increasingly been shown to be a critical part of effective reading. Good readers constantly monitor and check what they are understanding as they read a passage.

5 Semantic Mapping

Rather than memorizing isolated word lists, semantic mapping can be used as a foundation for building an effective personal strategy for acquiring new vocabulary knowledge.

6 Collaborative Learning

The opportunity for students to work together on various types of reading projects has shown itself to be an excellent technique for encouraging meaningful reading.

7 Word Processing

The use of word processing is only one of many new ideas and techniques in reading using educational technology. Currently, word processing has had the most positive effect on students' reading and writing based on programs using the computer.

8 Teacher Effectiveness

Techniques include time on task, questioning strategies, use of materials, and grouping procedures. The emphasis in this work has been on the fundamental role of the teacher as an instructional leader in the reading program.

9 Reading Aloud to Students

Teachers should include each day, along with sustained silent reading, a period of oral reading to their students.

10 Encouraging Lifelong Reading

The reading program that encourages students to become lifelong readers has been successful no matter what other activities are used. The ultimate goal of all reading instruction should be to develop in readers the need and the desire to let reading be a meaningful part of the rest of their lives.

Cathy M. Roller

UNIVERSITY OF IOWA

1   Read aloud to children every day.

2   Set aside a regular time each day for children to read and write.

3   Read and write yourself.

4   Set aside a regular time each day for children to talk about what they read and write.

5   Share your own reading and writing experiences with your students and your peers.

6   Replace worksheets and workbooks with reading and writing time.

7   Have a large classroom library.

8   Give children choice in what they read and write.

9   Have as your most important goal children's independence in reading and writing.

10 Stop quizzing children about what they read. Listen to their ideas and have real conversations.

Martha Rapp-Haggard Ruddell

SONOMA STATE UNIVERSITY, ROHNERT PARK, CALIFORNIA

1 The Directed Reading Activity (DRA)

The DRA (Betts, 1946) has permeated reading instruction for at least 30 years. Translated into the basic structure of the basal reading lesson—*preparation for reading, guided silent reading, comprehension development, skill development and application, extension and follow-up activities*—the DRA has been used, if not known by name, by generations of elementary classroom teachers, reading teachers, and some middle school, junior high, and senior high English teachers. Whatever one believes about its merits (and well taught, the DRA has many), we must acknowledge its influence and presence. The well-educated reading teacher should know it by name, and have at least some idea of what decade marked its appearance into the literature.

2 The Directed Reading-Thinking Activity (DR-TA)

The DR-TA (Stauffer, 1969) was intended to, and does, extend the DRA in a substantial and dramatic way. The DR-TA shifts the teacher's role from leader-questioner to leader-facilitator by changing the focus of teacher talk. Whereas the teacher once asked, "What were Dick and Jane trying to do in this story?" "Why did they feel the way they did?" "What would you have done?", he or she now asks (in the DR-TA), "What do you think will happen?" "What makes you say that?" "Now, what do you think?" and "Why?" The DR-TA engages students in precisely the kind of predict/read/repredict/read-some-more process that good readers use naturally. Reading teachers who use it, in whatever form, reinforce the good readers, and give not-so-good readers a chance to experience what good readers do.

3 Context-Structure-Sound Dictionary (CSSD)

Not nearly as well known as the DRA or DR-TA, CSSD was introduced by William S. Gray in his 1946 book, *On Their Own in Reading*, as a systematic approach for word analysis and word identification. I think it is unfortunate that this strategy is not well known, because it represents a solid, reasonable, *balanced* approach to word analysis that is just as useful today as it was 45 years ago; it provides readers with a workable system for answering the all-important question, "What do you do when you come to a word you don't know?"; and its use militates against the indiscriminate use of one-shot, sound-it-out-only strategies. The irony here is that, though little known, CSSD was just as institutionalized as the DRA in at least one basal reading series (Scott, Foresman). It is an important idea, and needs to be more widely known and correctly attributed.

4   The Vocabulary Self-Collection Strategy (VSS)

VSS (Haggard, 1982) is a radical approach to vocabulary instruction for two simple, powerful reasons: (1) It proposes that students, rather than teachers or textbook writers, choose the words that they (the students) are to study and learn more about. This stems from the premise that students learn easily and effortlessly those words they *need to know* and consider to be important to what they are doing (it also acknowledges the rather dismal record teachers and textbook authors have established in predicting which words students already know and which they don't!). (2) It proposes further that vocabulary instruction should follow, rather than precede reading. Here, again, the premise is pretty reasonable—good readers do not know what words they need to learn or know more about until after they have read. Neither does anyone else. Identification of words to learn follows naturally and sensibly *after* silent reading, and students enjoy participating in the word selection process. The idea *is* radical— people have to change some fundamental assumptions about how vocabulary is acquired and developed in order to accept it; nevertheless, VSS changes the face of "vocabulary instruction" in classrooms. What was once simply endured becomes an animated, avid, and lively search for more information about *words*. Reading teachers, and their students, benefit from its use.

Concepts

5   Informal Reading/Language Assessment

I include in this concept all of those things we associate with informal evaluation—the Informal Reading Inventory (Betts, 1957), miscue analysis (Goodman, 1970; Goodman and Burke, 1972), cloze testing (Taylor, 1953), Group Reading Inventories, holistic evaluation of reading and writing (Davidson, 1989; Calkins, 1986), and the notion of diagnostic teaching that encourages teachers to watch how students respond to instruction and make decisions based upon that response. I also include the innovation of publishing IRIs in spiral-bound 8 1/2-by-11-inch booklets with perforated pages for easy removal, reproduction rights granted by the author, and cost and administration time reduced because it made the IRI so useful to classroom teachers. To the best of my knowledge, this was first done with the *Classroom Reading Inventory* (Silvaroli, 1965). Reading teachers knowledgeable about the many aspects of informal assessment and experienced in their application are more likely to become the informed classroom decision-makers we all hold to be ideal.

6 Content Area Reading Instruction

The notion that one learns how to read subject matter textbooks best by learning such reading as one learns the content itself is a pretty powerful notion. It was also a pretty unsettling notion to subject area specialists when it was described in detail in Herber's *Teaching Reading in Content Areas* (1970); and, this notion's long-time presence in the literature notwithstanding, it's not all that popular among subject area teachers today. While there has been a lot of talk in various decades about "teaching reading beyond the elementary grades" (1920s), "Every Teacher a Teacher of Reading" (1970s), "learning to read/reading to learn" (ad infinitum), "reading across the curriculum" (1980s), and so forth, it was Herber's forceful rationale and clear delineation between developmental reading instruction and content area reading instruction that marked intensive effort on and growing acceptance of such a notion. It is now standard fare in the curriculum that comprises the reading/language field; it has yet to become part of the minds and souls of mathematicians, scientists, historians and poets. Reading teachers must be knowledgeable and articulate in content area reading instruction because they are the ones who educate subject area teachers and convince them to carry out their critical part in its implementation.

7 Schema Theory

Schema theory (Bartlett, 1932; Bransford and Johnson, 1972; Anderson, 1977; Rumelhart, 1981) has changed how we think and talk about the intellect, cognition, and organization of information. This, in turn, has caused us to reexamine, restructure, and restate our view of the reading process (and more recently, the writing process as well). Of real importance in this effort is that schema theory is unbiased; many different views or theories of the reading process are explainable in schema theory terms. Further, through its articulation, we have a clearer understanding of the role of prior knowledge in all literate and cognitive acts. Reading teachers with a working understanding of schema theory thus have a cohesive base upon which to develop their own theory of the reading/writing processes, a foundation for examination of new ideas and instructional strategies, and the basis for intelligent decision making.

8 Emergent Literacy

Emergent literacy (Teale and Sulzby, 1989), like VSS in the Instructional Strategies section, is relatively new; some might consider it precipitously included in the ten best ideas list. I don't. The notion of emergent literacy involves not only reading (Clay, 1975; Sulzby, 1985; Teale and Sulzby, 1989), but spelling developmental stages and invented spelling (Read, 1975; Henderson and Beers, 1980), writing (Clay, 1975; Teale, 1987), and all varieties of language use (Harste, Woodward, and Burke, 1984) as well. It is of signal importance if for no other reason than the fact that "emergent literacy" is quickly replacing "readiness" as our preferred means of conceptualizing and describing what happens developmentally before an individual achieves full-blown literacy. It is a much richer, fuller conceptualization that acknowledges explicitly the interrelationship of all language systems and that has clear implications for beginning reading/writing instruction. Reading teachers at all levels are enriched by a thorough understanding of this concept.

Events

9 The First Grade Studies

The First Grade Studies (Bond and Dykstra, 1967) were landmark research in a number of ways. First, they were certainly the largest coordinated research effort launched in the field of reading and language development—27 studies conducted with over 30,000 children in cities and towns of 17 different states; each study designed to compare two or more of 11 approaches for teaching first grade reading; and an overall design to account for as many demographic variables as possible. Second, they answered once and for all the question, "Can we determine the best way to teaching beginning reading by focusing our professional attention on comparison of specific methodologies (The Great Debate)?" The answer is no. While the full complexity of study findings cannot be addressed here, the most overriding conclusion drawn from The First Grade Studies must be that teachers, rather than methodologies, are the critical variables in determining student success in beginning reading. Thus, the third landmark aspect of the The First Grade Studies is that they demonstrated clearly that it was time for the Great Debate to end — for us to put aside niggling discussion of such non-issues as "phonics vs. look-say" and focus instead exactly where the combined studies directed us—on the teacher, the students, and the language and other interactions established in the classroom. To our benefit, we have done just that. Reading teachers with knowledge of this 25-year progression are well prepared to answer critics intent upon reviving the moribund debate, and to redirect discussion in terms of our current knowledge and understanding of reading/language instruction.

10 Publication of Theoretical Models and Processes of Reading

Publication of the first edition of *Theoretical Models and Processes of Reading* (Singer and Ruddell, 1970) marked a growing emphasis and attention on theory building in the field of reading. Much had been happening along that line during the decade of the 60s, and *Theoretical Models* was one of the first major theoretical publications. It was significant by its inclusion of diverse authors and various points of view, by its wide availability as a publication of the International Reading Association, and by its clear intent to stimulate interest and research activity rather than provide end-all, be-all answers. This intent has been achieved through three editions in which original articles have been revised and updated; new articles/theories/research have been added; and greater emphasis on connecting theory, research and practice is evident. Certainly, all reading teachers do not need to read everything in *Theoretical Models and Processes of Reading,* but they should know at least some of what it contains, because what it contains represents much of prevailing knowledge and points of view. With over 40,000 copies sold in its 20-year history, it has acquired the status of a cultural allusion. Knowledgeable people in our professional culture should know of its presence.

Author note: The citations used in my Ten Best Ideas are intended to document the entrance of these ideas into the literature. As such, they often represent authors' first words on a subject; I am well aware that later editions and iterations are more refined and generally the best words on any topic. My intent was to capture the history as well as the content of the ideas I chose.

Leo M. Schell
KANSAS STATE UNIVERSITY

1 Match child and book.

Repeated and long-term assignment to materials that are difficult to read produce dislike, disinterest, hostility, and eventually apathy in even the best students. Think what significant mismatches do to average and below-average readers!

2 Reading practice is more important than reading instruction.

Skills instruction and practice are important, but children learn to read more by reading than by practicing skills.

3 Automaticity in decoding aids reading comprehension.

Instantaneous recognition of words and quick use of decoding principles facilitate understanding of what is read. And the more a reader reads, the better she or he becomes at word automaticity. Skills practice isn't the only way to improve automaticity in decoding.

4 The amount of time spent in actual reading may be the most important factor in reading growth.

Many pre- and post-reading activities such as discussion, dramatization, and drawing may be counterproductive if they are too time-consuming and rob students of time for reading.

5 Reader interest in material and personal satisfaction from reading may be crucial factors in determining attitude toward and motivation for reading.

A wide variety of material at varied reading levels, time to explore and learn about them, and time to read and share them are essential.

6 The home environment may be as or even more important than the school or teacher in learning to read.

Relationships and communication between home and school deserve special attention.

7 Many different approaches, materials, and organizational plans

are currently in use but none seems decidedly best, although different ones may achieve some goals better than do others.

Therefore, know your goals!

8 *Student writing/composing seems to enhance reading achievement, particularly at the beginning stages of reading development.*

Time needs to be found for expressive personal writing and decreased time devoted to "fill-in-the-blanks" writing in language arts/English textbook exercises.

9 *The total amount of time devoted to the reading curriculum in the elementary school may be disproportionately large and may rob time from other curricular areas.*

In elementary schools, we have reading instruction (basals, novels, and so on), reading practice, independent reading (SSR), teacher oral reading, and pupil sharing. It's possible that the total amount of time devoted to all these different aspects forces other curricular areas to receive less time and attention than they deserve.

10 *A few children have a very difficult time learning to read and we're unsure why. Our best efforts seem to produce minimal, not optimal, growth.*

For some people, learning to read as well as the average reader in the population may be nearly impossible, and we may have to settle for slow growth. (But this shouldn't diminish our efforts!) If singing were as important in our society as reading is, how many of us would be assigned to Remedial Singing classes year after year after year? And how many of us would never reach "grade level" in singing achievement?

James Squire

GINN AND COMPANY EMERITUS

Select a short story that is somewhat ambiguous in its presentation of character, such as "The Hundred Dresses," by Eleanor Estes (middle grades) or "All the Years of Her Life," by Morley Callaghan (upper grades). Read the story to its climax, but stop short of presenting the ending to the class. Ask students a few open questions: What do they think the story is about? How do they think the main character feels? After exchanging diverse views for a few minutes, ask students to write several sentences predicting how the story will conclude. Then read the author's ending and ask students to compare it with their own predictions. Observe the clues which some readers perceived and others did not. Conclude the activity by eliciting from the class some observations on the ways in which the nature of a character in fiction influences the significance of what occurs.

Norman A. Stahl

NORTHERN ILLINOIS UNIVERSITY

Michele L. Simpson
Christopher Hayes

UNIVERSITY OF GEORGIA

1   The key to moving beyond the "basic skills" approach to college reading instruction and to gaining greater professional respect lies in adopting an academic orientation of the instructor as "learning specialist" rather than as only a "remedial/developmental" reading specialist. The learning specialist views his or her mission as one of assisting any and all students to become successful independent learners.

2   Learning specialists should utilize assessment devices that reflect the reading/study tasks students will be required to undertake in lower division courses. One way this can be accomplished is through a simulation of a typical learning experience. Each student's work is evaluated for both process and product. To evaluate a student's processes of study, the learning specialist merely reviews textbook markings (if any) and any other materials (e.g., notes or outlines) with the aid of a checklist of appropriate criteria. To evaluate the products of study, the objective and essay questions can be scored.

3   If students in a developmental studies program are not enrolled concurrently in a credit-bearing content-area course, consider teaching strategies through the simulation model. The goal of such a model is to replicate the tasks and texts of a typical lower division course that most students are required to take after the completion of the developmental education requirement. When the students exit the simulation course, they take with them a physical product (marked text and appropriate strategies), a cognitive product (greater prior knowledge and experience), and several domain-specific and general study strategies.

4   If students are concurrently enrolled in credit-bearing courses, group them into study triads focusing on classes that tend to cause problems. Throughout the term as the learning specialist introduces various generic learning strategies, each triad can modify the strategies to the

tasks and texts of their targeted course. Furthermore, the students can provide peer assistance and mentorship to each other by completing activities such as (1) cross-checking each other's lecture notes for accuracy and completeness, (2) peer-teaching difficult problems or concepts encountered in the lecture or text, (3) helping each other monitor and evaluate personal understandings of the course content, (4) preparing for exams by quizzing each other and listening to talk-throughs of major concepts, (5) debriefing each other after examinations, and (6) providing general emotional support.

5   College learning specialists must provide experiences that immerse the students in (1) the language of the academy or the jargon that allows the institution to function (e.g., terms such as *provost, bursar, financial aid*), (2) the educated or generally advanced vocabulary used by scholars as they communicate, and (3) unique technical terms and symbols of a discipline which permit scholars within a field to communicate effectively and efficiently. To help students master the vocabulary in category (1), draw heavily upon the institution's printed materials, particularly the college catalog. Generative vocabulary activities are suggested for developing greater fluency with vocabulary in category (2). Finally, students can promote independent learning of vocabulary in category (3) with Sartain's "Technical Vocabulary Log for Study Triads" or Simpson's "Concept Cards."

6   A promising comprehensive strategy entitled PORPE has been developed for instruction in textbook study systems.

With PORPE students are involved in Predicting potential essay questions to guide their studying; Organizing key ideas which answer those predicted questions and use their own words, structure, and methods; Rehearsing the key ideas; Practicing the recall of those key ideas in self-assigned essays; and Evaluating the completeness, accuracy, and appropriateness of the essays via a checklist.

7   The college learning specialist must meet the needs of students who have a deficiency in general and content-specific knowledge and many misconceptions about learning. Learning specialists can promote the habit of reading regularly and widely and the development of greater general knowledge and vocabulary through the creative use of periodicals such as *Newsweek* or *Time* during the weekly

classroom routine. Learning specialists can also provide higher-level background experiences while teaching students to learn about a specific theme or concept by utilizing or adapting Bartholomae and Petrosky's "Basic Reading/Basic Writing" model.

8   Experienced college learning specialists realize that many students enter required reading courses with a negative attitude about being assigned to a "remedial" class. Hence, begin by teaching a high-utility strategy that promotes immediate transfer to other course work. Instruction on how to take notes from lectures or from assigned readings provides such an avenue to immediate use.

9   Consider the use of undergraduate teaching assistants funded with work-study money, receiving independent study credit, or serving in an honorary society such as Phi Eta Sigma. These assistants should be successful students who possess an academic worldliness, a repertoire of efficient and effective learning strategies, and a desire to pass this insider knowledge on to another student. The teaching assistants can work with triads, small groups, or with individual students needing intensive assistance.

10 Be an active member of the college reading and learning community. Join the organizations that support our mission, such as the College Reading Association, the College Reading Special Interest Group of I.R.A., the National Association of Developmental Education, and the College Reading and Learning Association. Read the journals that carry articles related to our profession, such as *Reading Research and Instruction, Journal of Reading, Journal of College Reading, Journal of Developmental Education*, and *Forum for Reading*. Be an active member in our profession by presenting papers or delivering workshops at local, state, regional, and national conferences and by writing for publication in state and national journals, newsletters, and yearbooks. Finally, be a mentor to new college learning specialists by sharing materials, experiences, successful instructional strategies, and your "ten best ideas for college learning programs."

Jo Stanchfield

OCCIDENTAL COLLEGE, LOS ANGELES, CALIFORNIA

1   Learn all you can about the teaching of reading in the context of the language arts and try out new ideas within your own philosophical approach.

2   Send encouraging messages constantly to your students to let them know that they are valued, capable, and responsible.

3   Develop a structure for teaching both vocabulary and comprehension skills, based on previous levels of skills development. Use a variety of evaluative techniques to determine skill level. Be sure there is sufficient practice on the skill taught and adequate time for learning to take place. If the skill is not learned, *reteach*.

4   Use the dynamic theory of expectancy to help students develop higher and higher levels of competency by remarks such as, "I know you can do this task; I expect you to do it; and I'll help you." Let students know that everyone is a potential winner.

5   Plan your teaching to ensure that every student has at least one dosage of success every day. To do this, break your instruction into attainable learning units and give practice on what has been taught. Actively teach more and test less.

6   Practice an enthusiastic, positive, lively teaching style. These qualities, plus a warm smile, are magical and make the classroom come alive.

7   Arrange homework assignments to include from three to three and a half hours a week of easy, enjoyable reading. This practice, over a period of time, will lead to a level of automaticity in reading power.

8   Increase reading achievement by adding directed listening activities to directed reading activities. Use read-aloud strategies daily from children's and/or adolescent literature to increase vocabulary meanings, improve listening abilities, enhance critical thinking, and develop an awareness of the joy found in reading books.

9   Be knowledgeable about your students' interests and select books for them to read that challenge and excite them. This maxim applies also to the books chosen for read-aloud strategies. Especially, consider the reading interests of boys.

10 This above all, learn to love your students into learning. In the true meaning of an act of love, use words, tonal qualities, and body language that express warmth and build self-esteem in your students. Show that you care about your students by providing a nurturing environment in which they can learn.

Barbara Taylor

UNIVERSITY OF MINNESOTA

1   Give children time to read real books.

2   Show your excitement for and promote the reading of literature.

3   Teach children how to apply word recognition and comprehension strategies to independent reading of actual text.

4   Give children the opportunity to engage in higher-level thinking related to material they have read.

5   Integrate discussions and writing with the reading of literature unless the material is being read purely for enjoyment.

6   For the assessment of pupil progress, use daily reading tasks that do not break reading into discrete skills.

7   Provide special help (see number 3) for low-achieving readers as early as possible (the beginning of first grade is best).

8   Remain sensitive to individual children's needs and interests as developing readers.

9   Help children value reading for enjoyment and for learning.

10 Be a person who personally reads—for enjoyment and for learning.

Richard L. Venezky

UNIVERSITY OF DELAWARE

1   Keep a diary on reading instruction.
Write in it every day.
Index it at the end of each year.
Skim it at least once each month for ideas.

2   Visit reading clinics.
Observe.
Discuss.

3   Work in depth; do less, but do it better.

4   Bring in everyday literacy examples such as ads or posters at least once each week.

5   Ask students to read sentences backwards as a check on word recognition.

6   Ask students to keep a log for one week of everything they read outside of school. Discuss these in class.

7   End every day with a short reading: fiction, nonfiction, advertisements, jokes, and so on.

8   Collect books from everywhere. Fill the room with them.

9   Stress self-monitoring.

10   Teach about books and book handling (parts of books, kinds of books, printing techniques, editing, authoring, and so on).

Shelley B. Wepner
William Paterson College, Wayne, New Jersey

1 Progressive Writing

An adaptation of the Progressive Dinner, at which a group of people eat each part of a five-course meal in a different home, Progressive Writing promotes the same progressive movement in writing as groups of participants go from table to table to experience each writing stage. Each Progressive Writing step is described below.

a. (Prewriting) Have each group of students jot down words, such as *round*, related to an object on the table. (5 minutes) Entire group moves to the next table, which has a different object.

b. (Writing) Have each group write a story related to the new object,using the words or ideas written by the previous group during prewriting. (7 minutes) Entire group then moves to the next table.

c. (Revising) Have each group revise (add/delete/reorganize) the story written by the previous group. (7 minutes) Entire group moves to the next table.

d. (Editing) Have each group edit for mechanics (grammar and spelling) the revised story of the previous group. (5 minutes) Entire group moves to the next table.

e. (Creating Final Copy) Have each group create a final copy of the edited piece written by the previous group. (5 minutes) Entire group moves to the original table.

f. (Reseeing) Each group looks at the story created for its object and shares reactions.

2 Cubing

Cubing is a prewriting strategy that facilitates students' higher-level topical thinking for writing. Adapted by Kloss and Granger (1984), this strategy provides students with a six-sided viewpoint of a topic or object through six writing "prompts": describe it, compare it, associate it, analyze it, apply it, argue for or against it.

An adaptation of this technique is a personalized cube, encouraging students to share something about themselves in words and phrases.

3 Clustering

Clustering, a graphic representation of thoughts, ideas, and feelings, helps students to see relationships between facts and ideas and make connections between the new and the known. Often referred to as brainstorming, cognitive mapping, semantic mapping, or webbing, clustering is a verbal picture of ideas that are organized by the reader.

4 CAPER (Children And Parents Enjoy Reading)

CAPER is an at-home recreational reading project that requires parents to read *with* their children rather than *to* their children for 15 minutes every night. Each month, children take home a monthly progress chart so that both parents and children can indicate their amount and type of reading (e.g., newspaper, magazine, science fiction book) each day.

5 Reading Di-A-Logs

Reading Di-A-Logs are a combination of reading logs and dialog journals. "Reading Logs" provide an outlet for students' reactions to their daily reading. "Dialog Journals" are conversational journals that allow students to share their ideas, feelings, and concerns over time.

Reading Di-A-Logs combine these two ideas so that students have an opportunity to engage in conversation about mutually shared reading material.

6 Flowcharting

Flowcharting, pictorial representations of computer programs that use special symbols and arrows to create a "map" of what the computer will do, requires knowledge of a particular subject and an understanding of how to process the information. Flowcharts can be used as creative vehicles for expressing students' thoughts about daily events and ideas.

7 Reading with Environmental Logos

Environmental logos, used to advertise products with bold and colorful symbols featuring printed words in design format, make an indelible impression upon young children's memories. Familiar commercial logos (for example, McDonald's, Crest, Coca-Cola) should be used in a rebus-like fashion with ordinary words children know (for

(for example, *Mommy*, *Daddy*, *loves*, *likes*) to help them develop a beginning reading vocabulary.

8 Computerized Language Experience Approach

Using the child's natural language—a reflection of the child's syntactic knowledge, content knowledge, and interests—makes the child feel secure in reading print on the page. A computerized language experience approach provides a speech synthesized word processor with primary print so that students can have their thoughts recorded and then hear their thoughts spoken.

9 K-W-L and K-W-L Plus

K-W-L is a procedure for helping students to become active readers of expository text. Developed by Ogle (1986), this procedure consists of three basic cognitive steps: (1) accessing what I Know; (2) determining what I Want to learn; and (3) recalling what I Learned as a result of my reading.

10 Stratepoint

Stratepoint is a critical thinking technique for middle school/junior high students (Andreano and Wepner, 1989). Divided into seven questioning stages, this technique provides questions for students to ask as they make decisions about ideas, events, and problems.

Robert M. Wilson

UNIVERSITY OF MARYLAND

My ten best ideas come from a variety of sources but share a common theme: focusing on the strengths of students. When students experience difficulty with reading success, it is easy to focus on their difficulties and attempt to provide "correction." What these students need, however, is a series of success experiences so that they can enjoy the feeling of reading as something that they can do well.

1 Contracting for Student Success

Students should be permitted to make decisions about the nature of their learning in terms of content, strategies, and pacing. A simple contract can be negotiated with the student regarding the learning that is to be undertaken. When the contract is accomplished, the student is successful.

2 Cooperative Learning for Student Success

Students should be permitted to work together to achieve their educational goals. By working together, students often learn new strategies, produce better products, and stay on task better.

3 Starter Questions for Student Success

Lessons that start with personal questions tend to generate better answers than impersonal questions—that is, those that have only one right answer. Teachers can ask personal questions by asking students questions that have stems, such as:

What do you think was:

- most interesting?
- most important?
- worth remembering?

4 Personal Outlining for Student Success

Following the use of personal questions, students can use their answers to develop personal outlines by having them take their personally important idea and placing it in an outline form. Then they go back to the passage and find supporting information for their personal idea to complete their personal outlines.

1. _____
    Personally identified important idea

    a. _____
        Support

    b. _____
        Support

    c. _____
        Support

5 Signing for Vocabulary Success

Students who have difficulty retaining reading sight vocabulary often find it easy to remember their words when the words are introduced with signs in the following manner.

- Show the student the word.
- Show the student the sign for the word.
- Pronounce the word.
- Have students sign, then pronounce the word.
- Repeat several times.

Teachers need not know any signs to use this idea. They only need to have a sign book such as *The Comprehensive Signed English Dictionary* published by Gallaudet University Press. When a sign is needed, just look it up in the dictionary.

6 Webbing for Student Success

For many students, the use of a graphic aid such as webbing activates long term memory of passage information. A web of the information of these ten best ideas might look like the following:

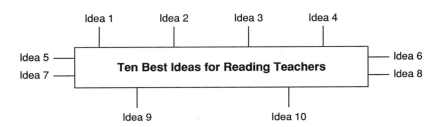

7 Circle Stories for Student Success

Another graphic aid can be the use of circle stories. On a blank segmented pie, students can draw picture of important story parts in each segment and place words or phrases on the outside of the pie for each of the pictured segments.

8 Task Analysis for Student Success

When students encounter serious difficulty with reading tasks, there seems to be an inclination to do some type of testing. Task analysis would be a better first step. The teacher simply identifies the problem, lists student strengths and weaknesses regarding this problem, and then plans several short lessons. Each lesson should use the student strengths and address one of the weaknesses. Quite often the answer to the difficulty can be determined without any testing.

9 Captioned Television for Student Success

By obtaining a caption tele-decoder teachers can use some of the hundreds of hours of closed-captioned television that are shown each week. Using the captions as reading materials while the students enjoy their favorite television shows is a novel way to provide for the incidental learning of sight vocabulary. Captions are words that appear on the bottom of the screen, making the TV show a moving story book, but they can only be seen if a caption tele-decoder is attached to the TV set.

10 Bookmarks for Student Success

Some students have difficulty remembering what strategies they should use, even when those strategies have been taught recently. By making bookmarks that list these strategies, students can be reminded of the strategies and use them while they are reading. The following example of a bookmark has been widely used in Maryland.

Comprehension System "8"

Before you read

Look
at title, picture clues

Think
about what you already know

As you read

Predict
what you think will happen

Picture things
in your mind

Question yourself
Does it make sense?

Read on
Use context clues

Reread
silently or out loud

Ask someone
who knows

Ruth Yopp and Hallie Yopp

CALIFORNIA STATE UNIVERSITY, FULLERTON

One hundred seventy-five elementary school teachers who had recently served as Master Teachers for student teachers from California State University, Fullerton, were mailed a letter that asked them to list their ten best ideas for teaching children to read. This group was selected because they are considered excellent teachers and because they influence new starts in the profession. Fifty-six teachers responded to the letter, a return rate of 32%. Of these respondents, 61% were primary grade teachers (grades K-3) and 39% were upper grade teachers (grades 4-6). This sample ranged in experience from three to forty years, with 75% having more than ten years experience. Fifty-two percent hold Master of Science degrees, most of them in Education.

Below are listed the ten most commonly mentioned ideas for teaching children to read. They are presented in order, beginning with the most frequently occurring response.

1   Motivation and Success

The Master Teachers overwhelmingly responded that providing students with motivating materials and involving them in a variety of interesting activities are critical to a successful reading program. They also noted that the teacher's own enthusiasm for reading and his or her ability to provide successful experiences that develop confidence in the children greatly influence how well young children learn to read.

2   Writing

Almost every teacher included as one of the ten best ideas the integration of writing into the reading program. They believe that students learn to read through reading what they write, and that students should write in response to reading every day. Specifically, suggestions included writing journal and log entries, making class and individual books, writing new endings to stories, and rewriting stories from different characters' points of view.

3   Drama, Art, Music

Many respondents recommended that teachers incorporate drama, art, and music into their reading program. Allowing children to dramatize stories is motivating and "makes stories come alive" for the children. The use of art "seems to help children create a better picture" of what is happening in a story. Reading lyrics to songs is fun, and reinforces reading skills.

4   Reading Aloud to Children

Reading aloud models good reading, teaches children to enjoy reading, and "spreads the joy of the printed word." No one is too old to be read to, according to this group of Master Teachers, and teachers at all grade levels should read aloud to their students every day. They should read to the children "as if it mattered," one teacher said, "as if story time were the most important part of the day, every day." Some teachers recommended reading short stories related to subject area studies to students throughout the day.

5   Vocabulary

Vocabulary development should be an important component of the reading program, with an emphasis on teaching students to determine meaning from context clues. Other comments included posting charts to reinforce vocabulary, discussion of unfamiliar words, creation of personal dictionaries, and the use of games to motivate students to learn new words.

6   Oral Reading

Students should be provided with many opportunities to read aloud. While many teachers simply recommended the use of oral reading as part of a good reading program, several suggested specific oral reading activities. Among these were having the students play teacher and read aloud to classmates or younger children, choral reading, and partner reading. Another idea was "echo reading," in which the teacher begins reading a selection and each child joins in until all the students are reading together.

7   Integrated Curriculum

Teachers believe that successful reading programs are those in which the entire curriculum is integrated. Reading stories about the Revolutionary War while studying that time period in social science is an excellent way to build background knowledge, reinforce concepts, and improve comprehension. Learning about inventions of the period and writing letters from Loyalists to their families in England further involve students in meaningful activities that evolve through the entire school day.

8 Phonics

Include phonics in beginning reading instruction to give the children tools that they will need to tackle new words. Many teachers cited the importance of building a strong foundation for reading development with phonics instruction. Several also noted that phonics should be only one component of beginning reading instruction, and recommended the use of literature and language experience activities as well.

9 Parent Involvement

Teachers, especially primary grade teachers, recommended involving parents in the reading program. They suggested that teachers introduce parents to the program at the beginning of the school year in an effort to make them partners in their child's education. Parents should be encouraged to read aloud to their children daily, to listen to their children read frequently, and to model reading at home by reading themselves.

10 Literature

As one teacher put it, "It is natural for a child to love good stories, to learn from good stories, and to be inspired by good stories." Therefore, a literature-based program is recommended. Teachers stated that students become more involved with novels than with basal reading selections and enjoy them more. Additionally, students are exposed to better writing when they read novels.

References

Alvermann, D., D. Dillon, and D. O'Brien. *Using Discussion to Promote Reading Comprehension*. Newark, Del.: International Reading Association, 1987.

Anderson, R.C. "The Notion of Schema and the Educational Enterprise." In R. C. Anderson, R. J. Spiro, and W. E. Montague (Eds.), *Schooling and the Acquisition of Knowledge* (pp. 415-431). Hillsdale, N.J.: Lawrence Erlbaum Associates, 1977.

_____, L.G. Fielding, and P.T. Wilson. "A New Focus on Free-Reading." Symposium presentation at the National Reading Conference, San Diego, California, December 1985.

_____, E.H. Hiebert, J.A. Scott, and I.A. Wilkinson. *Becoming a Nation of Readers: The Report of the Commission on Reading* (Contract No. 400-83-0057). Washington, D.C.: National Institute of Education, 1985.

Andreano, V., and S.B. Wepner. "Decisions, Decisions: Choosing the 'Write' Option." Paper presented at William Paterson College, Wayne, N.J., 1989.

Annis, L. F. "Student-Generated Paragraph Summaries and the Information-Processing Theory of Prose Learning." *Journal of Experimental Education*, Vol. 54 (1985), pp. 4-10.

Applebee, A. N. *The Child's Concept of Story*: Ages 2 to 17. Chicago: The University of Chicago Press, 1978.

_____. "Environments for Language Teaching and Learning: Contemporary Issues and Future Directions." In J. Flood, J. Jensen, D. Lapp, and J. Squire (Eds.), *Handbook of Research on the Teaching of the English Language Arts*. New York: Macmillan, 1991.

Armbruster, B. B., T.H. Anderson, and J. Ostertag. "Does Text Structure/Summarization Instruction Facilitate Learning from Expository Text?" *Reading Research Quarterly*, Vol. 21(3) (1987), pp.331-346.

Bartholomae, D., and A.R. Petrosky. *Facts, Artifacts and Counterfacts: Theory and Method for a Reading and Writing Course*. Upper Montclair,

N.J.: Boynton/Cook Publishers, Inc., 1986.

Bartlett, F. *Remembering*. Cambridge, England: Cambridge University Press, 1932.

Baumann, J.F. "A Generic Comprehension Instruction Strategy." *Reading World*, Vol. 22 (1983), pp. 284-294.

_____. "The Effectiveness of a Direct Instruction Paradigm for Teaching Main Idea Comprehension." *Reading Research Quarterly*, Vol. 20 (1) (1984), pp. 93-115.

_____. "Teaching Third-Grade Students to Comprehend Anaphoric Relationships: The Application of a Direct Instruction Model." *Reading Research Quarterly*, Vol. 21 (1986), pp. 70-90.

Bean, T. W., H. Singer, and S. Cowen. "Acquisition of a Topic Schema in High School Biology Through an Analogical Study Guide." In J. A. Niles and R. V. Lalik (Eds.), *Issues in Literacy: A Research Perspective*, Thirty-fourth Yearbook of the National Reading Conference. Rochester, N.Y.: National Reading Conference, 1985.

Berkowitz, S. J. "Effects of Instruction in Text Organization on Sixth Grade Students' Memory for Expository Reading." *Reading Research Quarterly*, Vol. 121(2) (1986), pp. 161-178.

Betts, E. A. *Foundations of Reading Instruction*. New York: American Book Company, 1946.

_____. *Foundations of Reading Instruction*. New York: American Book Company, 1957.

Bond, G. L., and R. Dykstra. "The Cooperative Reading Program in First Grade Reading Instruction." *Reading Research Quarterly*, Vol. 2 (1967), pp. 5-142.

Bransford, J. N., and M.K. Johnson. "Contextual Prerequisites for Understanding: Some Investigations of Comprehension and Recall." *Journal of Verbal Learning and Verbal Behavior*, Vol.11 (1972), pp. 717-726.

Buss, R. R., J.L. Ratliff, and J.C. Irion. "Effects of Instruction on the Use of Story Starters in Composition of Narrative Discourse." In J.A.Niles and R. V. Lalik (Eds.), *Issues in Literacy: A Research Perspective*. (pp. 55-58). Rochester, N.Y.: National Reading

Conference, 1985.

Calkins, L.M. *The Art of Teaching Writing*. Portsmouth, N.H.: Heinemann Educational Books,1986.

Carroll, J. B. "Developmental Parameters of Reading Comprehension." In J. T. Guthrie (Ed.), *Cognition, Curriculum, and Comprehension*. Newark, Del.: International Reading Association, 1977.

Casale, U.P. "Motor Imaging: A Reading-Vocabulary Strategy." *Journal of Reading*, Vol. 28 (1985), pp. 619-621.

_____, P. Davies, and B. Richman. *The American Heritage Word Frequency List*. Boston: Houghton Mifflin, 1971.

Chall, J. S. *Stages of Reading Development*. New York: McGraw-Hill, 1983.

_____. "Readability and Prose Comprehension: Continuities and Discontinuities." In J. Flood (Ed.), *Understanding Reading Comprehension: Cognition, Language, and the Structure of Prose*. Newark, Del.: International Reading Association, 1984.

_____. "Afterword." In R. C. Anderson, E. H. Hiebert, J. A. Scott, and A. G. Wilkinson, *Becoming a Nation of Readers: The Report of the Commission on Reading*. Champaign, Ill.: The Center for the Study of Reading and The National Academy of Education, 1985.

_____. "Reading and Early Childhood Education: The Critical Issues." *Principal*, 1987a, Vol. 66 (5) (1987a), pp. 6-9.

_____. "The Importance of Instruction in Reading Methods for all Teachers." In *Intimacy with Language: A Forgotten Basic in Teacher Education*. Baltimore, Md.: Orton Dyslexia Society, 1987b.

_____. "Two Vocabularies for Reading: Recognition and Meaning." In M. G. McKeown and M. E. Curtis (Eds.), *The Nature of Vocabulary Acquisition*. Hillsdale, N.J.: Lawrence Erlbaum Associates, 1987c.

_____, and M.E. Curtis. "What Clinical Diagnosis Tells Us about Children's Reading." *The Reading Teacher*, Vol. 40 (1987), pp. 784-788.

_____, V.A Jacobs, and L.E. Baldwin. *The Reading Crisis: Why Poor Children Fall Behind*. Cambridge, Mass.: Harvard University Press, 1990.

_____, and R.W. Peterson. "The Influence of Neuroscience upon Educational Practice." In S. L. Friedman, K. A. Klivington, and R.W. Peterson (Eds.), *The Brain, Cognition, and Education*. Orlando, Fla.: Academic Press, 1986.

_____, and C.E. Snow. "School Influences on the Reading Development of Low-Income Children." *The Harvard Education Letter*, Vol. 4 (1) (1988), pp. 1-4.

_____, and S.A. Stahl. "Reading Comprehension Research in the Past Decade: Implications for Educational Publishing." *Book Research Quarterly*, Vol.1(1985), pp. 95-102.

Clay, M. M. *What Did I Write?* Aukland, New Zealand: Heinemann Educational Books, 1975.

Clymer, T. "The Utility of Phonic Generalizations in the Primary Grades." *The Reading Teacher*, Vol. 16 (1963), pp. 252-258.

Dale, E., and J. O'Rourke. *The Living Word Vocabulary*. Elgin, Ill.: Dome, 1976.

Davidson, J. L. *Holistic Reading Assessment*. Monroe, N.Y.: Trillium Press, 1989.

Davis, F. B. "Research in Comprehension in Reading." *Reading Research Quarterly*, Vol. 3 (1968), pp. 499-545.

Duffy, G.G., and L.R. Roehler. "Characteristics of Responsive Elaboration Which Promote the Mental Processing Associated with Strategy Use." Paper presented at annual meeting, National Reading Conference, St. Petersburg, Florida, December 1986.

Duffy, G., L. Roehler, and J. Mason (Eds.). *Comprehension Instruction*. New York: Longman, 1983.

Durkin, D. "What Classroom Observations Reveal about Reading Comprehension Instruction." *Reading Research Quarterly*, Vol. 14 1978-79), pp. 481-533.

Eanet, M.G., and A.V. Manzo. "REAP—A Strategy for Improving Reading/Writing/Study Skills." *Journal of Reading*, Vol. 19 (1976), pp. 647-652.

Fielding, L. G., P.T. Wilson, and R.C. Anderson. "A New Focus on Free Reading: The Role of Trade Books in Reading Instruction." In T.E. Raphael and R. Reynolds (Eds.), *Contexts of Literacy*. New York: Longman, in press.

Fitzgerald, J., and D.L. Spiegel. "Enhancing Children's Reading Comprehension Through Instruction in Narrative Structure." *Journal of Reading Behavior*, Vol. 12 (1983), 1-17.

_____. "Textual Cohesion and Coherence in Children's Writing." *Research in the Teaching of English*, Vol. 20 (1986), pp. 263-80.

_____. "Improving Reading Comprehension through Instruction in Story Parts." *The Reading Teacher*, Vol. 39 (1986), pp. 676-82.

Flood, J. "The Text, the Student, and the Teacher: Learning from Exposition in Middle Schools." *The Reading Teacher*, Vol. 39 (1986), pp. 784-791.

_____. (Ed.). *Promoting Reading Comprehension*. Newark, Del.: International Reading Association, 1984a.

_____. (Ed.). *Understanding Reading Comprehension*. Newark, Del.: International Reading Association, 1984b.

_____, D. Lapp, and N. Farnan. "A Reading Writing Procedure that Teaches Expository Text Structure." *The Reading Teacher*, Vol. 39 (1986), pp. 556-561.

Fry, E. B. "Fry's Readability Graph: Clarifications, Validity, and Extension to Level 17." *Journal of Reading*, Vol. 21 (1977), pp. 242-252.

_____. "Reading Formulas—Maligned but Valid." *Journal of Reading*, Vol. 32 (1989a), pp. 292-297.

_____, D. Fountoukidis, and J. Polk. *The New Reading Teacher's Book of Lists*. Englewood Cliffs, N.J.: Prentice Hall, 1984.

Gambrell, L., W. Pfeiffer, and R. Wilson. "The Effects of Retelling upon Reading Comprehension and Recall of Text Information." *Journal of Educational Research*, Vol. 78 (March/April 1985), pp. 216-220.

Glass, G.G. *Teaching Decoding as Separate from Reading*. Garden City, N.Y.: Adelphi University Press, 1973.

Goodman, K. S. "Behind the Eye: What Happens in Reading." In O.S.

Hiles (Ed.), *Reading: Process and Program*. Urbana, Ill.: National Council of Teachers of English,1970.

Goodman, Y., and C. Burke. *Reading Miscue Inventory Manual*. New York: Macmillan, 1972.

Graves, M.F., M.C. Penn, and C.L. Cooke. "The Coming Attraction: Previewing Short Stories." *Journal of Reading*, Vol. 28 (1985), pp. 594-598.

Gray, W. S. *On Their Own in Reading*. Chicago: Scott, Foresman, 1946.

Greaney, V. "Factors Related to the Amount and Type of Leisure Reading." *Reading Research Quarterly*, Vol. 15 (1980), pp. 337-357.

_____, and Hegarty, M. "Correlates of Leisure-Time Reading." *Journal of Research in Reading*, Vol.10 (1987), pp. 3-20.

Guthrie, J. (Ed.). *Comprehension and Teaching: Research Views*. Newark, Del.: International Reading Association, 1981.

Haggard, M. R. "The Vocabulary Self-Collection Strategy: An Active Approach to Word Learning." *Journal of Reading*, Vol. 26 (3) (1982), pp. 203-207.

Hansen, J., and R. Hubbard. "Poor Readers Can Draw Inferences." *The Reading Teacher*, Vol. 37 (1984), pp. 586-589.

Harste, J. C., V.A. Woodward, and C.L. Burke. *Language Stories and Literacy Lessons*. Portsmouth, N.H.: Heinemann Educational Books, 1984.

Hayes, D. A., and R.J. Tierney. "Developing Readers' Knowledge Through Analogy." *Reading Research Quarterly*, Vol. 17 (1982), pp. 256-280.

Henderson, E. H., and J.W. Beers. (Eds.). *Developmental and Cognitive Aspects of Learning to Spell*. Newark, Del.: International Reading Association, 1980.

Herber, H. L. *Teaching Reading in Content Areas*. Englewood Cliffs, N.J.: Prentice Hall, 1970.

_____. *Teaching Reading in Content Areas* (2nd ed.). Englewood Cliffs, N.J.: Prentice Hall, 1978.

Holbrook, H. T. "Reader Response in the Classroom." *Journal of Reading*, Vol. 30 (1987), pp. 556-559.

Holmes, J.A. *The Substrata-Factor Theory of Reading*. Berkeley, California: California Book, 1953.

Ingham, J. L. *Books and Reading Development: The Bradford Books Flood Experiment*. Exeter, N.H.: Heinemann Educational Books, 1981.

Irving, A. *Promoting Voluntary Reading for Children and Young People*. Paris: UNESCO, 1980.

Johnson, D.W., R. T. Johnson, and G. Maruyama. "Interdependence and Interpersonal Attraction among Heterogeneous and Homogeneous Individuals: A Theoretical Formulation and a Meta-Analysis of the Research." *Review of Educational Research*, Vol. 53 (1) (Spring 1983), pp. 5-54.

_____, G. Maruyama, R. Johnson, D. Nelson, and L. Skon. "The Effect of Cooperative, Competitive, and Individualistic Goal Structures on Achievement: A Meta-Analysis." *Psychological Bulletin*, Vol. 89 (January 1981), pp. 47-62.

Kintsch, W., and T.A. Van Dijk. "Toward a Model of Text Comprehension and Production." *Psychological Review*, Vol. 85 (1978), pp. 363-394.

Kloss, R., and V. Granger. "Writing as Process Seminar." Paper presented at William Paterson College, Wayne, N.J., June 1984.

Langer, J. A. "Facilitating Text Processing: The Elaboration of Prior Knowledge." In J. A. Langer, and M. T. Smith-Burke (Eds.), *Reader Meets Author/Bridging the Gap: A Psycholinguistic and Sociolinguistic Perspective* (pp. 149-162). Newark, Del.: International Reading Association, 1982.

_____. "Examining Background Knowledge and Text Comprehension." *Reading Research Quarterly*, Vol. 19 (1984), pp. 468-481.

Lapp, D., and J. Flood. *Teaching Students to Read*. New York: Macmillan, 1986.

_____, J. Flood, and N. Farnan. *Content Area Reading and Learning* (dedicated to Harry Singer). Englewood Cliffs, N.J.: Prentice Hall, 1989.

Long, H., and E.H. Henderson,. "Children's Uses of Time: Some Personal and Social Correlates." *Elementary School Journal*, Vol. 73 (1973), pp. 193-199.

Manzo, A.V. "The ReQuest Procedure." *Journal of Reading*, Vol. 13 (1969), pp. 123-126.

———, and U.P. Casale. "Listen-Read-Discuss: A Content Reading Heuristic." *Journal of Reading*, Vol. 28 (1985), pp. 732-734.

———, and U.C. Manzo. *Content Area Reading*. Columbus, Oh.: Merrill, 1990.

Meyer, B. J. F., D. H. Brandt, and G.J. Bluth. "Use of Author's Textual Schema: Key for Ninth Graders' Comprehension." *Reading Research Quarterly*, Vol. 16 (1980), pp. 72-103.

Moffett, J. *Teaching the Universe of Discourse*. Boston: Houghton Mifflin, 1983.

Morrow, L. M. "Home and School Correlates of Early Interest in Literature." *Journal of Educational Research*, Vol. 76 (1983), pp. 221-230.

———, and C.S. Weinstein. "Increasing Children's Use of Literature Through Program and Physical Design Changes." *Elementary School Journal*, Vol. 83 (1982), pp. 131-137.

Ogle, D. "K-W-L: A Teaching Model that Develops Active Reading of Expository Text." *The Reading Teacher*, Vol. 9(6) (1986), pp. 564-570.

Palincsar, A.S. "Reciprocal Teaching of Comprehension Fostering and Comprehension Monitoring Activities." *Cognition and Instruction*, Vol. 2 (1984), pp. 117-175.

———. "The Role of Dialogue in Providing Scaffolded Instruction." *Educational Psychologist*, Vol. 21 (1-2) (1986), pp. 73-98.

———, and A.L. Brown. "Reciprocal Teaching Activities to Promote Reading with Your Mind." In E.J. Cooper (Ed.), *Reading, Thinking and Concept Development: Interactive Strategies for the Class*. New York: The College Board, 1985.

_____, and A.L. Brown. "Interactive Teaching to Promote Independent Learning from Text." *The Reading Teacher*, Vol. 39 (1986), pp. 771-777.

Peabody, M. B. "The Effect of Concrete Examples on Transitional and Formal Students in the Instruction of Chemical Bonding." Unpublished doctoral disseration, Northern Arizona University, 1984.

Pearson, P.D. *A Context for Instructional Research on Reading Comprehension*. Center for the Study of Reading, University of Illinois, Urbana, 1982.

_____. "Changing the Face of Reading Comprehension Instruction." *The Reading Teacher*, Vol. 38 (1985), pp. 724-38.

_____, and M.C. Gallagher. "The Instruction of Reading Comprehension." *Contemporary Educational Psychology*, Vol.8 (1983), pp. 317-44.

Pearson, P.D., R. Barr, M.L. Kamil, and P. Mosenthal (Eds.). *Handbook of Reading Research*. New York: Longman, 1984.

_____, and D.D. Johnson. *Teaching Reading Comprehension*. New York: Holt, Rinehart and Winston, 1978.

Raphael, T. "Question-Answering Strategies for Children." *The Reading Teacher*, Vol. 36 (1982), pp. 186-190.

_____. "Teaching Question-Answer Relationships, Revisited." *The Reading Teacher*, Vol. 39 (1986), pp. 516-522.

Read, C. *Children's Categorization of Speech Sounds in English*. National Council of Teachers of English Research Report No. 17. Urbana, Ill.: National Council of Teachers of English, 1975.

Robinson, H. A., V. Faraone, D. Hittleman, and E. Unruh. "A Review of Trends and Research." In J. Fitzgerald (Ed.), *Reading Comprehension Instruction, 1783-1987*. Newark, Del.: International Reading Association, 1990.

Rumelhart, D. E. "Schemata: The Building Blocks of Cognition." In J. T. Guthrie (Ed.), *Comprehension and Teaching*: Research Reviews. Newark, Del.: International Reading Association, 1981.

Salisbury, R. "A Study of the Transfer Effects of Training in Logical

Organization." *Journal of Educational Research*, Vol. 38 (1934), 241-254.

Sartain, H.W., et al. *Teaching Techniques for the Languages of the Disciplines.* Pittsburgh, Pa.: University of Pittsburgh and the Fund for the Improvement of Postsecondary Education, 1982. (ERIC Reproduction Service Number: ED #234-653)

Schmidt, M. C., and D. O'Brien. "Story Grammars: Some Cautions about the Translation of Research into Practice." *Reading Research and Instruction*, Vol. 26 (2) (1986), pp. 1-8.

Shepherd, D. *Comprehensive High School Reading Methods* (Third ed.). Columbus, Oh.: Merrill, 1982.

Silvaroli, N. J. *Classroom Reading Inventory*. Dubuque, Ia.: William C. Brown, 1965.

Simpson, M.L. "PORPE: A Writing Strategy for Studying and Learning in the Content Areas." *Journal of Reading*, Vol. 29 (1986), pp. 407-414.

_____, S.L. Nist, and K. Kirby. "Ideas in Practice: Vocabulary Strategies Designed for College Students." *Journal of Developmental Education*, Vol. 11 (1987), pp. 20-24.

Singer, H. "Active Comprehension: From Answering to Asking Questions." *The Reading Teacher*, Vol. 31 (1978), pp. 901-908.

_____, and S. Beasley. "Motivating a Disabled Reader." In M. P. Douglass (Ed.), *Claremont Reading Conference Yearbook* (pp. 141-160). Claremont, Calif.: Claremont Graduate School, 1970.

_____, and D. Donlan. "Active Comprehension: Problem-Solving Schema with Question Generation for Comprehension of Complex Short Stories." *Reading Research Quarterly*, Vol. 17 (1982), pp. 166-186.

_____, and D. Donlan. *Reading and Learning from Text*. Hillsdale, N.J.: Lawrence Erlbaum Associates, 1985.

_____, and D. Donlan. *Reading and Learning from Text* (2nd ed.). Hillsdale, N.J.: Lawrence Erlbaum Associates, 1989.

_____, and R.B. Ruddell (Eds.). *Theoretical Models and Processes of*

Reading. Newark, Del.: International Reading Association, 1970.

Slater, W. H., M. F. Graves, and G.L. Piche. "Effects of Structural Organizers on Ninth Grade Students' Comprehension and Recall of Four Patterns of Expository Text." *Reading Research Quarterly*, Vol. 20 (1985), 189-202.

Smith, L. C. "An Evaluation of Studies of Long Term Effects of Remedial Reading Programs." Unpublished doctoral dissertation. Cambridge, Mass.: Harvard Graduate School of Education, 1979.

Stauffer, R. *Directing Reading Maturity as a Cognitive Process*. New York: Harper & Row, 1969.

Sulzby, E. "Children's Emergent Reading of Favorite Storybooks: A Developmental Study." *Reading Research Quarterly*, Vol. 20 (1985), 458-481.

Taylor, B. M., and R.W. Beach. "The Effects of Text Structure Instruction on Middle Grade Students' Comprehension and Production of Expository Text." *Reading Research Quarterly*, Vol.19 (1984), pp. 134-146.

Taylor, W. "Cloze Procedure: A New Tool for Measuring Readability." *Journalism Quarterly*, Vol. 30 (1953), pp. 415-433.

Teale, W. H. "Emergent Literacy: Reading and Writing Development in Early Childhood." In J. Readence and R. S. Baldwin (Eds.), *Research in Literacy: Merging Perspectives*. Rochester, N.Y.: National Reading Conference, 1987.

_____, and E. Sulzby. "Emergent Literacy: New Perspectives." In D. S. Strickland and L. M. Morrow (Eds.), *Emerging Literacy: Young Children Learn to Read and Write*. Newark, Del.: International Reading Association, 1989.

Thorndike, E.L. *The Teacher's Word Book*. N.Y.: Bureau of Publications, Teachers College, 1921.

Thorndike, R.L. "Reading as Reasoning." *Reading Research Quarterly*, Vol. 9 (1973-74), pp.135-147.

Tierney, R.J., and J. Cunningham. "Research on Teaching Reading Comprehension." In P.D. Pearson (Ed.), *Handbook of Reading Research*. New York: Longman, 1984.

Tobias, S. "When Do Instructional Methods Make a Difference?" *Educational Researcher*, Vol. 11 (4) (1982), pp.4-9.

Vygtosky, L.S. *Mind in Society: The Development of Higher Psychological Processes*. M. Cole, V. John-Steiner, S. Scribner, and E. Soubermann (Eds. and Trans.). Cambridge, Mass.: Harvard University Press, 1978.

Walberg, H.J., and S.L. Tsai. "Reading Achievement and Diminishing Returns to Time." *Journal of Educational Psychology*, Vol. 76 (1984), pp. 442-51.

Wong, J. A., and K.H. Au. "The Concept-Text Application Approach: Helping Elementary Students Comprehend Expository Text." *The Reading Teacher*, Vol. 38 (1985), pp. 612-618.

Wood, P., J. Bruner, and G. Ross. "The Role of Tutoring in Problem Solving." *Journal of Child Psychology and Psychiatry*, Vol. 17, pp. 89-100.

Index of Names